HR TRANSFORMATION

Lead Your Business into HR 3.0 and Beyond

Dr. Wade Larson

Copyright ©2021 by Wade Larson. All rights reserved. Printed in the United States of America. Except as permitted under the United States Copyright Act of 1976, no part of this publication may be reproduced or distributed in any form or by any means or stored in a database or retrieval system without the publisher's prior written permission.

ISBN 9798500051356

Design by Greg Larson

For more information, visit www.WadeLarson.com

To Lauri and all your inspiration.

See Dr. Wade's other titles available through Amazon.

Doing HR Better

Mind Shifts in Healthcare

Contents

Forward vii
Staying Ahead of Change 1
HR 2.0...It's Time to Move On 11
HR 3.0: The Need for a Transformation 21
The Elements of HR's Transformation 41
Transforming the Delivery Model 49
Digital Transformation 75
People Transformation 101
Change Leadership 141
Management and Strategy Development 163
Cultural Transformation 181
HR Professional: Personal Transformation .. 213
Where to Start 223
About the Author 247
Citations 249

Forward

Through the decades, we have seen a divergence of thoughts, attitudes, and perspectives. The workplace has become far more complicated. As I began my career 25 years ago, things were crazy then. Little did I know we were just getting warmed up.

In the '90s, HR attempted to transition from a traditional administrative focus – what we'll refer to as HR 1.0. "Personnel Management" focused on paperwork, compliance, and organizational process as the way to manage people and jobs.

We shifted our emphasis to people as the primary resource for any organization – the *human* resource. We built partnerships with managers to achieve business strategy. Our *strategic* approach then moved us to HR 2.0. As strategic business partners, we focused on streamlining processes, centralizing services, building relationships, and helping managers and leaders succeed.

Over the past two-and-a-half decades, we've partnered with executives to achieve business strategy. Some companies did better than others. As we worked as a field to evolve, the world around us changed quickly, and there is no sign of it slowing down.

We have been fighting a war for talent that shows no sign of letting up. With fewer people in the workplace, fewer entering into critical fields, and a lower number attending college and trade school, the war for talent appears to have just started.

Businesses now face more significant levels of competition. Our organizations must apply agile at every level and process. The need to use resilience, flexibility, and adaptability has never been greater. The speed of change requires employees to develop new competencies continually and pivot no matter their position.

Globalization has created a 24/7 work environment that creates new pressures to get more done. It also changes the work dynamics, talent requirements, and acquisition challenges to find the right solutions.

Digital connectedness has demanded faster service, improved technology, and a focus on innovation. HR has felt the pressure beyond streamlining to include full-scale digital transformation to enhance employee performance and service capability.

By themselves, each of these pressures is enough to require HR to reimagine how to deliver its promise. These pressures combine to demand that HR reinvent itself.

Yes – we still have administrative functions to perform, but we can streamline and outsource them.

Yes – we are still strategic business partners, but that partnership has evolved.

It's time for a new approach.

What is HR 3.0?

HR 3.0 is about doing this differently to meet the demands of today's new workplace realities. Our businesses have changed. The world has changed. Our employees have changed. It's now time for HR to make the same type of change to keep up and get ahead so it can lead the change.

This book looks at six major areas affecting businesses and HR today and their role in the foreseeable future. After scouring the research and trends, the six most prominent drivers of today's HR priorities are identified and discussed. At the heart of these priorities is the HR professional.

We discuss each of these areas and the role of the HR professional and what it will take to be successful moving forward. Doing the same things over and over expecting different results is not productive. (Remember the definition of insanity?) Continuing to stick to your guns of HR 2.0 – a 25-year-old model and philosophy – will keep you in the past. It's time to evolve to the next level of your success.

I invite you to join us in this exploration of what it will take moving forward. While I do not pretend that every one of these topics or examples will apply to each person, department, organization, or situation, I am confident that the topics we discuss will spark an idea or conversation to begin your improvement process.

Whether you implement a concept from this book or it inspires you to start a different transformation that ultimately takes you to a better place, I hope you find your success!

Here's to *your* success!

Dr. Wade

x

Staying Ahead of Change

The world of HR is...well, different. The world that we are working in is also different. Things have changed dramatically over the past several years. They've changed considerably over the past decade. They've changed significantly over the past year. The range of change has increased exponentially, and the demands placed upon us to keep up the pace of change have increased like never before.

HR is now called upon to not only keep up with that change but to drive it.

Do you recall those memes on social media that display images with captions reading "What My Friends Think I Do," "What My Mom Thinks I Do," and so on until "What I Really Do"? There is much truth to that – except it depends on the day.

Every day is unique to HR – never the same day twice. That is what makes it such an exciting area of the business. Nowhere else does any single function have so much *potential* to make such a big difference in the company's people, outcomes, and profits.

HR is tied directly into the people, practices, and leadership of any business. These are at the very core of operations, revenue generation, and strategy regardless of your industry or customer base. Without people, you have nothing. When we understand and use our human resources effectively within the business structure, we optimize our potential to achieve our best as individuals and organizations.

The challenge we face is the continued inability to transition the "potential" to "actual" performance. We want to be quick to blame the economy, the environment, global politics, or anything other than to look at ourselves. The truth is that we rarely find a situation that is 100% externally driven. Even in the darkest times, cases emerge where organizations pull together to emerge victorious and triumphant. They call upon their people to develop innovative strategies and approaches to adjust to the "new normal" and make it work.

Consider businesses' response to the 2020 pandemic. Almost overnight, the companies that pivoted found themselves shifting anywhere from 20-100% of their entire workforce from on-premises to remote. This was a massive undertaking coordinated by IT, operations, and human resources. HR had to lead the way to shift managers' mindsets. It was OK to allow flexible working hours, segmented schedules to allow for kids' needs (e.g., helping with home school and parental needs), and allowing for the occasional kid or dog in the Zoom call. Cultural acclimation from a staunch hyper-corporate standard to a "new normal" of virtual workspaces created a new reality that only HR could lead. Yet, even HR was challenged as they had to manage these changes remotely themselves. This became an opportunity for the prepared HR leaders to shine.

Our ability to adapt and pivot within our environment is tied mainly to our strategies and practices related to people, operations, and leadership. Success in these moments tends to be tied less to capital or tangible resources – less about the "what" – and more to "how" we use them. It requires an expert level of insight and adeptness by HR to guide executives and employees through the maze of confusion to achieve new levels of success.

Reality Check

We have the position to make a difference. We've been handed the keys to the castle. What are we doing with them?

It's now well into the 21st Century. Are we doing things differently than we were 10, 20, or even 30 years ago?

Think about it.

Consider our hiring practices. We have different technology, the laws have changed, and we try to promote greater cultural sensitivity. But at the end of the day, are we hiring people better or faster than we were a decade ago? Better yet – rather than measuring "time to hire," what about time to proficiency? Are we getting people into their jobs and helping them become proficient any faster?

Look at our candidates. Everyone applies online, yet most experience the same process as everywhere else they use. Is it the same experience they've had for the past decade of filling out the same questions, receiving the same information, cutting and pasting the same answers? Or are we discovering what we need to help us match the right people to the right positions at the right time?

Once hired, employees are there for more than just a paycheck. They expect an *experience*. The *Employee Experience (EX)* demands that we do things differently. Our employees have fundamentally shifted the way they think, work, and live. They're smarter, faster, and more flexible, resilient, and dynamic than ever before. Are we?

For those of us who have been around for a while, we have seen the "waves" of HR transitions. We shifted from an administrative focus of "Personnel" management to a new dynamic of Human Resource Management. The likes of Dave Ulrich challenged us to become a *strategic partner* to challenge this brave new world and forge new alliances to address the shifts in the workplace. We saw the evolution through the previous waves shifting first from administration to HR practices, then on to strategy, and finally on to HR and a future-ready context. We've talked a great talk. Many have walked it.

As a profession, we're at a point where we must pause and evaluate. Despite the great efforts and leaps taken, are we where we need to be? For example, one study finds that HR professionals are still spending 86% of their time on administrative "stuff." Wow! That doesn't sound like we're changing.

This may sound like an overgeneralization and does not apply to every HR professional, but it remains the stigma we face as a profession. The stigma would not still exist after the past two decades if we weren't doing it. It's time for us to take an honest look at what we do, why we do it, and how we can make a radical difference in the lives of those we serve.

Why We Still Do What We Do

HR is the first to criticize others' lack of ability to make changes, impeding functions throughout the business, and not seeing the big picture. It's time to look in the mirror. HR is one of the most challenged when it comes to all of these. We (as a function) take on an elitist perspective that gets in the way of others within the organization, and to be honest – we get in the way of ourselves.

Consider these perspectives:

- Is HR a "place" or a "function"? If people in the business talk about HR as a person or a place, we're doing it wrong. HR professionals don't "do" HR...we support HR functions. The frontline managers hire, fire, promote, etc., and are the ones *doing* HR...we are building and supporting the function to facilitate it.

- Are HR professionals stuck in the office? If people *come to* HR, then how can HR get to know whom they serve? Nothing will alienate HR faster than a "come to us" service model or orientation.

- Do you find yourself spending more time working on HR or *in* HR? It gets easy to fall into the trap of the contributor. As HR leaders, we still see endless paperwork. We think that if we can jump in to help, we'll get through it faster and then get back to the strategic 'stuff' later – but never do. The administration is our Zen, and we are reluctant to let it go.

- Are you quick to default back to your contributor role? Would you rather crunch numbers and run an analysis than step up to the front of the room and speak out against a wrong decision in a room of fellow executives?

- When you attend meetings, are you the first to pull out the notebook and volunteer to take minutes? Do your colleagues simply assume that you'll take notes and serve as secretary for the group because that's what HR does?

- Is HR invited to the meeting proactively or preventatively? If HR is at the meeting, are they there to develop ideas on winning or achieving tremendous success? Or are they there to keep the project or idea out of trouble? That's the difference between a "strategic" business partner and a risk mitigator.

- What is our response when the CEO hands down organizational change? Are we upset and resistant because they didn't consult with us first? Or do we adapt like any other group? (An elitist mentality tends to spend time wondering why they didn't consult them.)

- Do you see others as needing to change – rather than you? Do you talk about how others are the problem or why others cannot conform to *your* policies and procedures? Do you see your approach as being the best or the only way most of the time?

- Do you include other managers into your HR strategy sessions or pass ideas by other colleagues related to getting their input or feedback? Or do you keep it to yourself, thinking that you're the only one qualified to develop HR strategies?

- Are we still helping employees work through new employee "orientation"? Or do you deliver a unique employee *experience* that continues through their entire employment?

- Do you see employees as *human resources*? Or a *partner* to help the business achieve its goals?

Your honest response to some of these questions will help you recognize your position. Our behaviors dictate our viewpoint. We often find that we do things to ourselves – if we find ourselves struggling to feel empowered to make changes, we must first change ourselves.

We ask others to be open and reflective during the change process. If we in HR are not available for self-reflection, evaluation, and collaboration, how can we expect to progress?

Time to Move Away from the Hamster Wheel

Consider the hamster wheel. That poor little guy is in there running faster and faster – I'm not sure where he's going, but he's making great time. Do you feel that way in HR?

We keep spinning around thinking that if we go faster – crunch more data, process more forms, and develop more policy, we'll create a better world. As I attend conferences, workshops, seminars, and meetings, we still talk about the same things. The books still talk about the shift to strategic partnerships and business consultants. It's a good idea – don't get me wrong. But it's SSDD – Same Stuff, Different Day.

Many have succeeded in implementing these strategic business partnerships, and HR is a functional asset to the bottom line. Several HR leaders caught the vision, made the shift, and have transformed their work environments into the platform conducive to delivering the employee experience that today's talent demands. If so, you're in good shape. To the other 85%, it's time to move on to something new.

If you are in the early stages of HR – what we may refer to as HR 1.0, where you focus on the administrative role – I invite you to stick around. We'll talk about a new model to consider that can take you leaps and bounds into the future. You do not need to move through HR 2.0 before you get to HR 3.0. You can simply jump ahead and become an HR 3.0 operation following the model provided in our discussion.

For those who operate in the HR 2.0 model – the strategic business partnership model – I also invite you to stick around. We share a model to help you upgrade to the latest approach to meet the demands of today's workforce. Things have changed over the past 25+ years since we made a fundamental shift in the world of HR. It's time to adapt to the needs of today's workforce and deliver the best experience possible.

Finally, those HR functions that have taken steps to adopt HR 3.0 practices, I welcome your thoughts and considerations. As we continue to forge our way into the new world, there will be much to learn. We will apply new models, identify what works (and what does not), and collaborate at an entirely new level. This calls for the sharing of best practices.

HR 2.0...It's Time to Move On

Before the 1990s, we were in what we'll call "HR 1.0." It was very much the Personnel Department, focused primarily on the 4-P's: policies, processes, payroll, and paperwork. People were in there somewhere, but primarily as something that we just processed and managed. This function oversaw hiring, firing, discipline, filing, and processing employee data. It was rarely used for strategic purposes unless data was needed on employment, such as turnover rates, time to hire, or market conditions. (We still see several HR departments focused on compliance, administration, and efficiency.)

Enter the changing workplace.

While the workplace of the early 1990s had shifted a bit, things were essentially business as usual. Some progressive companies began to recognize the value of managing employees proactively and turning the role into a strategic function. For the most part, however, it took a few significant catalysts to shake up our world:

- Major sexual harassment lawsuits arose during the Clarence Thomas Supreme Court hearings as his former assistant, Anita Hill, took the stand to talk about her experiences. As the nation listened, it opened the floodgates of litigation as others recognized that they no longer had to put up with bad behavior. Compliance took on new significance.

- Economic shifts took place as we expanded into a global economy by removing trade borders (e.g., *NAFTA*), worked through recessions, and created new business collaborations. Budgets became leaner, strategies became more profit-focused, and administration had to become aligned.

- The technology grew through the internet and cell phones. Information availability and global communication became instant, connecting the world like never before. We became a connected planet. Business required the same kind of connectedness to ensure internal communications among employees.

- Attitudes shifted. Gen X had taken to the workplace after having seen the downsizing of the '80s. No longer did companies automatically hold the loyalty and commitment of employees. They dealt with a free-agent workforce that was mobile, smart, technologically savvy, and they had options. Retention became important.

Dave's Model

It was 1997, and I was attending one of my first significant conferences as an HR professional. Being relatively new to the field, the speakers' names didn't stand out to me. As I listened to the keynotes, a speaker named Dave Ulrich took the stage – and it was exciting. Dave shared principles from his book about HR, strategic partnerships, and more. I thought that was just how we did it. I have not stopped listening to Dave since. Even today, with his latest models, he's still contributing and changing the HR world.

Dave provided a model for HR transformation[1] that has been used for many years to guide us from *traditional* HR into a strategic business partner model. This became our shift into the Golden Age - a transition from Personnel to Human Resources: "HR 2.0."

This transformation meant to shift HR into a strategic partnership with management. The goal was to treat people for what they are – the company's most important resource. If we treat them as such, we can use them much more effectively and optimize outcomes.

Like most models, it was a guideline to help us create a context for the conversation as we considered our shift into what has been our platform for the past era.

---

1 Ulrich, D. (1996). *Human Resource Champions.* Harvard Business Review Press.

Like thousands of others, I read and listened to Dave. I found many of these principles applicable as I created new perspectives that helped move us ahead. Now that we are well into the 21st Century, we need to consider our current evolution concerning this model.

Employee Engagement

The role and meaning of employee engagement have changed dramatically over the past several years. While we could say that the objective of employee engagement is similar, the nature of the employees themselves is substantially different. When Dave wrote his material, we were considering how to deal with integrating us, Gen Xers. Gen Z is completely different from that group, and whatever comes next will be at an entirely new level. Throwing in a global pandemic and changing economic models, working patterns, and individual needs creates a new dynamic for employee engagement that requires a different perspective.

Employee engagement has become fully integrated. Life is life. In the past, we would hear things such as "leave your personal life at the door." Easy to say, impossible to do. We recognize that our personal lives and work lives are intertwined. We can't shut off the fact that we have kids just because we came to work – or the challenges of life outside the workplace. The world has evolved to encompass a holistic approach that makes it impossible to separate segments of life. As a result, employees are searching for more than a simple paycheck in exchange for hours of servitude. They are looking for an experience that is congruent with their values, lifestyle, and needs.

Change Agent

For the past few decades, we have worked under the impression that we could actually "manage change." I, for one, follow the teachings of Peter Drucker as he shared that we cannot manage change but only get in front of it. An actual change agent drives it – we can either change or be changed. HR has continuously been sitting off to the side as a consultant to managers telling them *how* they should change or *what* they "ought to" change. However, rarely have they been out there in the thick of it at the forefront making the change happen. HR needs to shift from the Change Agent to the Change Driver – HR must *create* the change that drives the business.

Administrative Expert

The fact that we are even talking about this anymore makes me cringe. Yet, so many HR functions still spend a disproportionate amount of time talking about forms, processes, and procedures. We still spend an unholy amount of time talking about documentation, the need for details, and whatever the attorney told us to do. Yes, I understand the need for detail and precision when it comes to compliance. However, we don't need to spend 86% of our time dealing with administrative functions. There are three things that we must focus on: automate, automate, and automate. When we automate, we shift our attention to our business's actual needs, free up the time of our managers and employees, save much money in time and efficiencies, and enhance the employee experience. Automation of administrative processes has one of the fastest ROIs if done correctly.

Strategic Partner

This title of "Strategic Partner" has changed the mindset of many HR professionals. This has helped us to take giant leaps forward as a profession. Unfortunately, we are still acting as consultants. Instead, we need to take on full ownership. We need skin in the game. A business partner is better than we were before, but those who are still acting as consultants are still operating in the safety of their silos. It's time to get out of those silos and get a stake in the results, which means having some risk to the rewards. I am not saying that being a strategic partner is terrible – I am just saying that we can step up our relationship into a full-contact sport.

The HR 2.0 model was good. I think it was an exceptional model, and I respect Dave as the leader that pulled us out of the dark ages to lead us through a Renaissance to where we are today. (Thanks, Dave! His current work is still extraordinary and aligns well with our transition through HR 3.0.)

Did it work?

That is for us as individuals to answer. Like anything else, it depends upon what we did with it. I find that individuals who understood their business integrated HR strategically, applied the principles effectively, and led HR to be very effective. Those looking for a silver bullet to cure everything, or a secret recipe that would make everything work, were and still are disappointed. They typically have fallen into survival mode and are probably still at the same functional level as HR was 30 years ago. Except for some technological advances that just come with the territory, HR may still be the same as before HR 2.0.

When we first began to implement HR 2.0, we tossed around terms such as "having a seat at the table," denoting our need to be there with the rest of the executive team discussing the needs of the business. We said this is though we had not been there before – and in most companies, HR had not. Unfortunately, when we started using this language, I recall believing that it was a right rather than a privilege that needed to be earned. You see, there was a reason that we had not been invited in the first place. Once we were at the table, what did we talk about? The other executives talked about P&L, market strategies, customer acquisition, and new product development. We showed up and started talking about annual sexual harassment training, the company picnic, and how many managers had not completed their performance appraisals last month. See the difference? Are we still doing the same thing?

Most HR leaders took the ball and ran with it. Many caught on and forged alliances with senior executives to ask them what HR could do to help them be successful. We became strong partners in helping to achieve the mission, vision, and goals of the organization. We became trusted partners, consultants, confidants, and strategists. We worked to align the organization where individual goals contribute to the department or functional purposes, which, in turn, contribute to company goals. Together, everybody is on the same page, working in the same direction to accomplish the same thing.

This model has worked well as a guide for over 20 years. It set a standard that helped us recognize that we need to work like any other function in a business – we need to deliver value. Unless HR demonstrates a clear value in which we carry our weight and contribute to the bottom line, we will never be recognized for our role.

Despite our many efforts, many still see HR as an overhead expense or an administrative burden. HR is still a force to be *overcome* within the organization – a hindrance rather than an ally. Are we? Is this just another administrative cost? Or do we genuinely have an ROI?

Today's workforce is different. It's impossible to group the entire "workforce" into one "group." With five active generations in the workplace, it's impossible to create a one-size-fits-all approach to modeling. Additionally, employee attitudes, assumptions, perspectives, and goals are not just limited by generation – they span across age groups, career ambitions, and demographics.

We also see different perspectives about our people. While people are still the most valuable resource for a business, they are more than that. They **ARE** the business. (We already spoke to that.)

The topic of DEI (Diversity, Equity, and Inclusion) is also different from when we shifted to HR 2.0. Our primary focus was to avoid lawsuits. The hot topic of the day was sexual harassment. Today, sexual harassment claims have not slowed down, but we are back to the topics of racial inequities, social justice, and corporate culture as the primary drivers. While somewhat related, these have entirely different agendas.

Then when you throw in a pandemic, shift anywhere from some to all of your workforces into a work-from-home model, regulate who can come to work (and not come to work), and coordinate labor, HR takes the stage more prominently; managing in the "old ways" won't cut it. Innovative businesses adapted to the situation. Other companies did not and no longer exist. Much of it came down to how they handled their people's concerns.

HR has never been more complex, challenging, exciting, or necessary. However, if we continue to work as we did when we shifted to the HR 2.0 model decades ago, we cannot presume to believe that we will be equipped to face the current challenges facing organizations.

Like all models, it's time to evolve. We worked through the Renaissance of HR 2.0 – and it was good. It's now time to go through our next HR Revolution. Much like the Industrial Revolution, HR needs to understand its potential and make the next significant breakthrough to optimize its results. As it does, we will see new creations, new inventions, and new successes as we align people, strategies, and business results.

So... on to the Revolution.

HR 3.0: The Need for a Transformation

It has never been more important for HR to transform as a function.

The previous model (HR 2.0) was appropriate for that stage in HR's evolution. We moved to an integrated approach using centers of excellence, focusing on training and business partnerships. We delivered services at the point of need according to the organizational model. It was a good model – a better model than we had.

Today, we live in a world of global connectivity, talent management, and digital transformation. HR is still trying to manage the chaos of change from behind, and it's no longer working. The new world requires a different approach that allows HR to lead the change.

It requires a shift to HR 3.0.

First – HR 3.0 is not coming. It's already here. The world has completely changed. Design thinking has altered how people and organizations integrate with resources, production, and customers to solve problems and develop solutions. Design thinking has redefined employee expectations and created a human-centered approach to impact the employee journey from onboarding through development, performance, rewards, and off-boarding. How employees interact with their environment, technology, culture, coworkers, managers, and clients is entirely different – it's completely human.

Structured resource-based thinking thinks of people in terms of human resources – something that we've phrased as "the organization's most valuable asset." In an HR 3.0 design thinking model, the employee is at the center of it all. They are not *an* asset. They are *the* asset.

HR 2.0 helped us to become proficient at managing the person as a resource – which we had not done before – and for us in HR to shift into an institutional leadership role. HR 3.0 now focuses on optimizing outcomes by helping people reach their best through aligning talent, resources, goals, and organizational priorities. This requires a commanding presence to influence, organize, and drive these pieces to design more engagement, enhance innovation within the culture, and increase overall performance to achieve tremendous success.

This kind of shift requires much more than gradual, incremental changes. Sure, strategic partnerships and our role as change agents place us in an ideal position to make the shift. If we have built a robust organizational design, excellent leadership development, and support a broad culture that can support ongoing agility and innovation, you're already in a great place. If not, you have some work to do. Even if you head in the right direction, there are other parts to master, such as measuring employee engagement, creating a complete learning environment, implementing people analytics, digital HR, workforce management, and design thinking.

HR must create a massive shift in its approach to keep up with the times. Remember – the world has already changed. It's time to transform to get ahead of the change curve and start to drive the outcomes you want.

What Does HR 3.0 Look Like?

Researchers from groups such as IBM[2], McLean[3], and SAP[4] have explored characteristics of what HR 3.0 includes to meet the needs of today's workforce. Recognizing the need to focus on the employee's personal experience and to create processes centered upon the worker, HR 3.0 must consider the following elements:

- More Personalization: The world of on-demand media, customization and ordering has created an expectation of individualization. Regardless of headcount, each person expects a personalized experience throughout their employment experience. It is what some call Human Experience Management (HXM). This promotes specific talent management, digital

---

2 https://www.ibm.com/downloads/cas/0LR4N1WK
3 https://go.mcleanco.com/download-confirmation-f21
4 https://www.hcamag.com/au/specialisation/change-management/are-we-on-the-verge-of-hr-3.0/146407

engagement, diversity and inclusion, and other personalized responses.

- Implement Agile: HR must follow what other areas in the organization have already adopted. They must implement agile practices for more incredible speed and responsiveness to employees.

- Data-Driven: HR must integrate people-based data analytics to drive better and more accurate decisions throughout the organization. As the organization becomes more employee-dependent in its productivity, managers will become more dependent on data-related people. HR must develop and deliver those analytics.

- AI: A natural marriage of agile + data analytics integrates AI throughout HR to increase efficiency and speed of service to employees, primarily through faster self-service opportunities, digital transformation, and responsiveness.

- Deliver HR Where It Is Needed: HR must take on more of a consultative role. In previous models, HR is where you *go*. HR 3.0 offers a resource that is available where it is needed. HR becomes a function, not a department.

- Greater Transparency: More data, more access, and more significant "touch" require more openness to allow employees to maintain trust and reduce reputational risk if processes fall to secrecy and non-communication.

- Greater Professional Demands for HR: The HR Team must be more competent – both individually and collectively. HR professionals must know more as practitioners within their craft and seamlessly deliver new solutions faster to their organizations.

The business has been driven by Porter's three-legged stool of competitive advantage calling for "better, cheaper, faster" as the differentiators of any company to survive and thrive. The same call is made for HR as it drives forward to compete and thrive in the new world.

A Call for Transformation

You may wonder how transformation differs from "change." Isn't it the same thing? Hardly.

Change calls for us to do something different, often driving a few modifications or incremental improvements. A transformation calls for us to stop what we're doing and to start being something completely different. You've seen the hotel that changes brand names, but nothing on the inside has changed – the colors are the same, beds are the same, and even the staff is the same. Only the name has changed. Then you see the property that has been purchased and shuts down for a few weeks or months as the crews come in, the property is all but torn down and rebuilt, and it looks like a new building under a new hotel name. When you walk in, it is an entirely different experience. The first example is a "change"; the second example is a "transformation."

Most of us have gone through some sort of change management process. We've implemented new systems, followed new rules, or established new practices. Some changes were more favorable than others.

When we implement change, we are seeking different behavior. We seek different results. Because behavior generates results, we can simply force compliance to create this change. That can make a short-term change and perhaps even lasting changes in procedures (e.g., enter through the south door instead of the east door from now on). Much of this is penalty driven where behavior is motivated to avoid a penalty, pain, or something otherwise deemed suboptimal. Mostly, these are evaluative and non-emotional reasons.

It is finding ways to optimize talent – to dig deep into the soul of an employee and get to new levels of performance – that takes more than simple rote change. It requires commitment and change at the emotional level. Shifting mindsets, values, and beliefs is not easy. Under normal conditions, the first hiccup will drive most change initiatives back to the status quo. To make change stick, it will take a complete mind shift.

Looking back to my youth, my dad gave me two rules before I could drive: pay for my insurance and earn my Eagle Scout. I made it a point to reach my Eagle before I was old enough to drive. I was also highly motivated to earn my keep, so I started mowing lawns at ten years old and delivering newspapers at 12. By 14 when I could drive (in

Idaho!), I was working all summer and could pay the whopping $147! Ouch. That was real money.

By the time I was 16, I had been driving regularly. Dad told me to drive safe and not speed – bad things could happen, but I wasn't quite aware of what they were. Then I got my first speeding ticket, and I had to pay for it myself. Lesson learned – well, the first lesson. Then came the 6-month mark for my insurance. Dad made me pay for the impact on his insurance rates. I couldn't believe I had to pay an extra $200 per year now!! That more than doubled what I had been paying the entire year! Dad let me know that because it would stay on my record for 3-years, I would be spending the higher rate for that long. Wow!!

While I had heard him before, I was now ready to listen to what Dad was talking about. He informed me what would happen with our rates if I got ticket #2, and I didn't like the prospect. He also shared what ticket #3 would do to me. Ultimately, he would kick me off the insurance, and I would still have to pay him for the impact on his rates.

This shifted my mindset, which then naturally affected my long-term behavior. Before this incident, my behavior was driven by compliance as I tried to avoid what had been described but not emotionally felt. After this, I was emotionally impacted by paying the penalty myself, and I shifted my mindset to avoid the pain of future tickets. I was committed to changing my behavior. As a result, I have had far fewer speeding tickets than I would have had.

Results come from continued, lasting change. Compliance-based behavior change only lasts so long – and it can also only ensure that behavior merely meets the extent of the rules. The outcomes will never rise beyond the regulation limit (we don't give extra credit for being more compliant). Also, when others perceive the rule is not being monitored or is gone, the behavior will slip.

The Foundation of Lasting Change

Mindset is the foundation of lasting change. It changes the beliefs and values to identify what is possible, probable, and expected. As depicted below, it lays the foundation upon which all results are built.

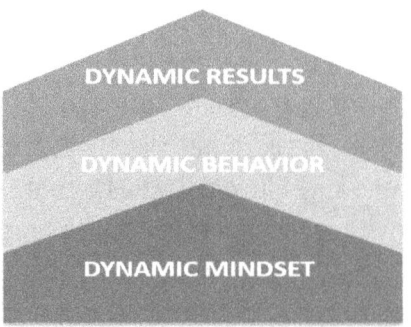

Typical change processes implement behavior-focused outcomes. Change happens, but it happens in small bursts. As a result, we suffer from change exhaustion. We use expressions such as "fake it 'til you make it." I know I'm guilty of it. We believe that if we create muscle memory by going through the motions enough times (behavior), the results will just happen. Some results will happen – that's the law of repetition.

Unfortunately, most of us fail to get in enough repetitions to make the behavior stick. Why? We're not committed. Unless we change the mindset first – our belief system – we will fail to maintain the behavior to create the results.

What We Know About Change

We begin most change management cycles with excitement, well-structured plans, and plenty of hype. We may make progress, gain momentum, and eventually see results drop. We push our efforts one or two more times, but ultimately, the steps plummet and the initiative fails. A little later, we try it again and we may make it a little farther. Then it happens again, sometimes failing even worse than the time before.

TYPICAL CHANGE IMPLEMENTATION CYCLE

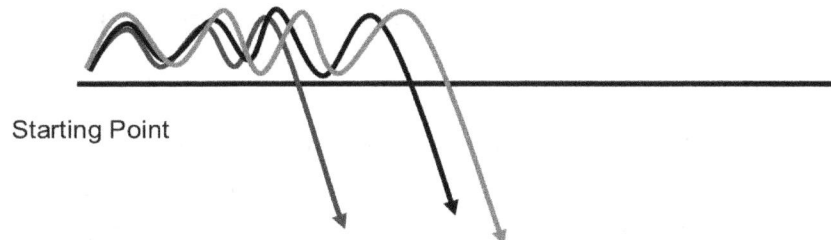

This cycle gets old for both us and employees. After a few change initiatives, employees simply recognize them as the "program of the month" and will wait you out. Even your employees in HR will need more than a simple change to shift from HR 2.0 to what comes next. In other words, change management alone won't be enough to take you to the next level.

Why does this cycle happen? Let's share a few things we know.

- Everyone *wants* to become "better," but they don't want to change or like change. You cannot have "better" without change – but employees won't naturally want to do what it takes to achieve the outcomes. *Imposing* changes (even if it is sold as *helping*) is usually resisted.

- Generally, people hate to *be changed*, but they don't mind changing if they think it's their idea. Any kind of shift in the way you think and behave that appears to be a top-down approach will be met with resistance. The best results are implemented from the ground up – you change what you need to change first and then tell people you changed it later after realizing that things are better.

- The longer someone has engaged in a habit or a process, the more difficult it is to change that habit. When it appears that you are making something *different* than what they know, they will resist. If you can show how the new way is similar to *but better than* the old way, they will buy into the change more readily.

- Following the principle of *homeostasis*, we are physiologically built to resist change. We fight to maintain the status quo. Even if we do change initially, our brains and bodies are wired to fall back to our comfort zones. Lasting change must be relearned. Transformational efforts require education, support, and reinforcement before, during, and after the change.

- Initial changes are effortless. Lasting transformation is complex. It must be learned, relearned, and reinforced time and time again.

Getting to a new way of doing HR will require more than a simple change management initiative. As we introduce HR 3.0, history shows that you may be shot down as just another program. Approaching the "leap" to HR 3.0 as another change management initiative will have similar results. We need something different that will shock the system enough to jolt you into a new way of operating.

Bringing in "The Quantum Leap Strategy"

Author Price Pritchett wrote a short book describing what he calls "The Quantum Leap Strategy."[5] Rather than taking several short, incremental steps to get from your starting point to the desired behavior, why not simply stop what you're doing and start behaving like you want to?

---

5 Pritchett, P. (1991). *The Quantum Leap Strategy*. Dallas, Tex: Pritchett & Associates.

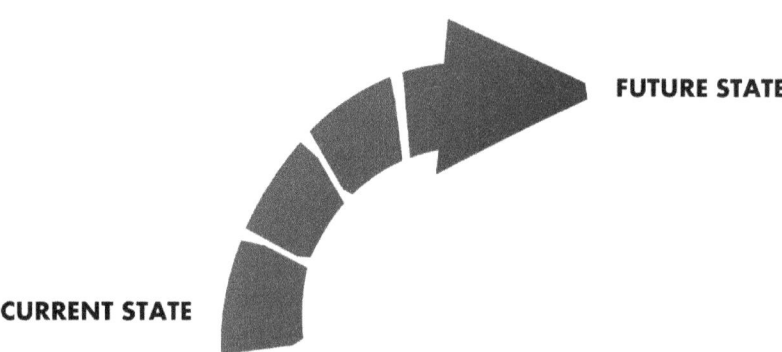

FUTURE STATE

CURRENT STATE

It becomes a commitment and a complete shift from how you do it today to the way you need to be. Quantum Leaping skips many steps tied up with day-to-day change management. There is no negotiating, no hesitancy, no dragging our feet, and no room for resistance. We simply stop doing what we were doing and start doing what we need to. This requires a change in our mindset, behaviors, and strategies as we stop doing what we were doing and start doing what we need to.

Admittedly, some processes must go through a series of changes that require steps of process improvement. For example, we cannot simply adopt "digital transformation" by walking in tomorrow and flipping the switch to using a new HCM system for our data management. However, we can "flip the switch" in our attitudes, mindset, and problem-solving approaches that will fundamentally alter how we lead the HR function. This type of transformation can happen in a moment as we adopt an outward mindset, shift our perspective from "obstacle" to "opportunity," and move into an action-oriented approach.

New ideas will abound as you recognize approaches available to you. New solutions to old problems will emerge. It's time to step into a new world and move away from the cliché of *thinking outside of the box*. As a friend of mine would say, we throw the box away.

Quantum Leaping Your Transformation

Achieving a transformative level of change will require a holistic mindset that results in the desired behavior changes.

Change	Transformation
Modifies Behavior	Modifies Beliefs & Values
Fixes the Past & Present	Defines the Future
Tactical & Operational	Aligns Strategy with Operations
Methods & Processes	Mindset
External Influence Driven	Internal Influence Focused
Goal: Improve Current	Goal: New System Optimization
Series of One-Time Efforts	Integrative, Holistic Approach
Top-Down Driven	Engages All Levels
Stable, Predictable, Defined	VUCA as the Norm

For HR to succeed in the new world of HR 3.0, it must take on different responsibilities.

- HR can no longer be the place where employees *come*. HR is no longer just a department – it must be a function or a service that integrates with everything and everyone throughout the business.

- People have consistently been recognized as valuable, but never so much as now. A shift in focus that manages talent using competency-based job descriptions and performance creates greater flexibility and opportunity for both the organization and employees.

- An employee-centric experience demands an integration using AI and systems to allow individuals to "build their adventure" where their role, background, and qualifications determine their onboarding, development, and employment experience.

- HR can enhance efficiencies and the end-user experience by integrating technologies such as augmented reality in interviews, training simulations, and customer interactions for performance evaluation and competency development.

- We can no longer take a one-size-fits-all approach to HR processes. Instead, we must design systems, pay, benefits, jobs, and the overall experience to match individuals where they are.

- HR leaders must become data-driven decision-makers to enhance access to managers for production-level decision-making.

- Diversity and inclusion have shifted from compliance to strategic competitive advantage in its role as HR helps to unleash potential through high performance.

Of course, these changes cannot happen overnight if you are currently operating at a level 1.0 or 2.0. Understanding where you are is essential. Recognizing where you want to go is just as critical. Every journey has a starting point and a desired destination. You will need to define your two points on the map.

Steps of Transformation Preparation

Your transformation process will be different from any other change management approach from the past. Sure, there may be similarities, but pay attention to some of the critical preparatory steps as you engage in the process.

I suggest the following five steps.

Step 1: Define Your Current HR Model

To determine where to go, you must first understand your starting point. Start by defining your current HR operating model. Describe two perspectives – HR as a department and HR as a function.

HR as a department is identified within the scope of the organization – where it falls in the organizational hierarchy, its reporting structure, access to executives and leadership, access to employees, etc. HR as a function is an evaluation of your processes, policies, and procedures. These are functions executed by your managers and employees and may include systems, methods of delivery, programs, and more. Consider the following:

- What are your current processes, procedures, operations, and hierarchical placement?
- How is HR perceived within the organization?

- How do employees and managers perceive HR practices?
- What is the current state of the business?
- What is HR's current role in helping the business achieve its goals?

Any current information provided from employee surveys, HR audits, or other data points may be useful at this stage.

Step 2: Vision and Focus

Change for the sake of change is generally a waste of time, energy, and resources. You must understand what you want, why you want it, and how to get there. The first step is to consider what you want from the transformation. This requires setting a vision of your goals, desired outcomes, and other details that can be clarified through questions such as these:

- What is the focus of your business, and how does HR want to support it?
- Is your HR function architecture established correctly to support the business?
- Is your service model the right one (to optimize the business' service delivery model)?
- Why do you want to make the change? What do you hope to achieve?
- What do you need to do to validate your change? What must you demonstrate as a result of your transformation to add greater value? (To whom must you demonstrate the value?)

Step 3: Desired State

Consider the desired end-state of the transformation. Define and describe your desired outcomes as clearly as possible. This will help you and your team recognize what "good" looks like and what you are trying to accomplish.

- What do you want HR to look like because of this transformation?
- How do you want HR to operate – both as a function and as a department?
- What do you want your team to know, be, or do differently because of this transformation?
- What benefits will result from your transformational journey?
- How will this add value to your business?

Step 4: Roadmap

Next, build your roadmap and begin the process. One challenge of transformation is doing something for the first time that is VUCA (volatile, uncertain, complex, ambiguous). In a change situation, you typically have control over the outcomes. You often know what you want to be changed, the degree to which you want to change, and precise measurements to define progress. In transformation, you may have a general direction, some great ideas and rely upon leadership to begin the process. It can be messy.

That's why you start with a vision and build a transformation plan – a roadmap to follow along the journey. Remember the adage that *failing to plan is planning to fail*. This is never truer than in transformation. While you cannot plan every detail, you must set up some guidelines.

As someone who enjoys working with youth, I believe in being prepared when I take a group of Scouts on a hike. Having worked with youth for decades, I recognize that anything can happen. Anything. I can't take everything with me, but I can take a few things to be prepared. I also acknowledge that while we have a map and general directions, things happen on the trail that are unexpected. If we know the general direction we are headed, we will move forward, overcome obstacles, and get there—the same works for HR transformation.

The transformational leader plans to get their team up the mountain, knowing that there may be obstacles and adjustments to be overcome along the way. There is no such thing as a perfect plan or the ability to predict everything. What you don't want is to be the leader that says, "Let's all show up at the trailhead at some point. When you get there, I'll point you in the general direction and give you some ideas on what to put into your backpack." That's just a bad idea. Unfortunately, it's how most transformational change efforts begin. It's also why most transformational change efforts fail.

Step 5: Execution

The rest of our conversation will focus on implementing your plan. It's great to build a program, talk about it, and draw out contingencies, but unless you take that first step to make changes, nothing will happen. The roadmap is built for you and your team to implement, evaluate and measure progress along the way, make adjustments as you progress, and guide your team to reach your destination. Taking the initial steps and maintaining your momentum to stay on course are the two most common reasons for HR transformation failures. Just getting started and continuing your transformation journey sets you up for success.

The Elements of HR's Transformation

Let's get specific when we start talking about the HR transformation. I shared that Dave's model was great for HR 2.0. So, what do we do about HR 3.0?

HR needs to build the platform strong enough to cover today's challenges and those that lie ahead in the future. The global HR function has been disrupted – and more disruption is on the way. It's time for a radical reinvention of the way that we do HR. Today's workplace calls for a radical shift in HR strategy, systems, processes, and technology.

Many HR leaders are already underway in making these changes. Some have direction. Some are trying to fake it as they look for solutions. Consultants are out on the marketplace selling their transformational miracles, but as we dig deeper, many of them are still talking about the same content we've seen for the past 20 years.

Today's focus on the employee experience is pivotal to the transformational process. The faster HR can move away from its administrative functions through process automation, AI integration, and streamlining, the more time it can focus on what matters most. According to a survey conducted of business leaders by IBM[6], five predictive indicators that drive success in the HR 3.0 environment include:

- A highly personalized employee experience focused on the individual.
- Competency-based approaches to building individual and business functions.
- Data analytics and AI at the core of decision-making.
- Incorporating principles of lean and agile to enhance service and response rates.
- Increasing openness and transparency of HR practices to improve trust.

While many HR functions may incorporate one or more of these areas into their current priorities, where is the organization with all five of these on its current list of action items?

Enter a New Model

To help us focus on how to achieve new results, bring in a new model. Like any other model, it provides a broad direction for you to apply to your business. *How* you adopt,

---

6 Accelerating the journey to HR 3.0.
https://www.ibm.com/thought-leadership/institute-business-value/report/hr-3

adapt, and use the model will depend upon your business model, needs, employees, and resources.

There are six primary areas of emphasis in the required HR 3.0 transformation, all aligned with the business's core objectives and clustered around one center of gravity: the HR professional. Recognizing that HR does not work independently, this model represents the specific focus within HR - emphasizing the people, practices, and leadership. HR's support of business goals and its engagement with other departments, employees, and leaders throughout the organization are understood but not represented in this model.

Let's take a look at the model.

HR 3.0

Cultural Transformation
Change the culture, change the momentum, change results

Strategy Development
Identify what you want, why you want it, and how to get it

Change Leadership
Be the leader in the room, step up, and do what it takes

Delivery Model
Take HR to employees – where they are, when they need it.

Digital Transformation
Automate, automate, and automate more to get more done.

People Transformation
Employees must make the shift to meet today's demands.

Beginning in the middle, the HR professional is central to the transformation. Without the individual's competencies, capabilities, talents, energy, and support, they will never be a fully engaged team member who can help create the complete transformation. With a fully engaged team, the identified six areas are critical to the preparation, engagement, and advancement of your success both now and in the future.

A brief description follows of each point.

One: The HR Delivery Model

HR must consider the model they use to deliver services to employees throughout the business. Whether the services are centralized, localized, following a center of excellence approach, or using some other design, it's time for an evolution of how programs, practices, policies, procedures, requirements, and HR business is done throughout the organization.

Manufacturing, operations, and business delivery have mainstreamed lean and agile models. HR must apply these same principles.

Two: Digital Transformation

Regardless of how much HR thinks they have automated systems, they must automate even more. The focus on the employee experience demands that we find more time to engage them directly. We can do it more intelligently – not harder. To do this, we need to reduce our administrative burden even further, eliminate processes where possible, and find ways to connect with employees more effectively. These call for a digital solution integration. It's not just about upgrading your systems – it's about a wholesale change, if needed, to save time, save money, and improve the employee experience.

Three: People Transformation

Employees want more and need more from their employment relationships than just a paycheck – they need the entire experience. We compete with their personal life for attention and commitment. They count on us for financial security as well as professional growth, development, and personal success. This requires us to become more competent and understand how to provide solutions more effectively to increase employee engagement, satisfaction, retention, and performance.

Four: Change Leadership

We have been managing change for years – we are no strangers to it. However, this becomes a mitigation strategy. The change is already happening. We are left to react and respond to the outcomes. We typically wait for somebody else in the organization to make the decisions, hand them down, and we are there to process and pivot as needed. HR needs to take on a different role by getting in front of the change and driving the outcomes. Following the motto "change or be changed," it's time to move from strategic partner to strategic leader.

Five: Management and Strategy Development

HR has generally seen itself charged with professional development. This includes management and leadership development, typically in the form of training courses and leadership preparation. It's time to step it up to fully engage strategic workforce planning, alignment with business strategy and integrate it with career and professional development among employees, managers, and leaders alike. Without a fully integrated plan, we will continue to train managers in a vacuum and gain the same results.

Six: Cultural Transformation

HR is not a stranger to culture change. We typically drive change initiatives to influence behavior through policy implementation, programs, or engagement activities. Taking on a new attitude about change, leadership, and ongoing development is a very proactive approach. This requires a shift in mindset among executives first. It also requires an alignment between their communications, corporate language, and promotions to ensure that the desired culture is identified, plans are created, and that HR leads that transformation.

The HR Professional
At the center of this transformation process is the HR professional. As mentioned previously, without the heart, mind, and soul of that person, anything done within this model will simply be a change to behavior without the total commitment required to make the successful shift. Even if

there are marked improvements initially, rarely does it create lasting change without full commitment. This central component includes a personal transformation that aligns with the functional adaptation of this process.

The rest of this book will center around each of these principles of transformation as they apply to today's HR. As we work our way through the book, consider where you and your team are in your evolution. What steps can you take to move to the next level? What must you start doing that you currently are not? What must you stop doing now? What can you continue to do and continuously evaluate moving forward?

Transforming the Delivery Model

HR delivers several services to the organization. Payroll may or may not be processed out of HR, but HR plays a role in time and attendance, processing timesheets, and/or several other related functions. HR manages employee benefits, hiring, performance management, talent acquisition, workforce planning, and a long list of other things.

Structurally, HR as a department is typically centralized, decentralized, or works in an account management structure.

- Centralized: HR is generally located in one place.

- Decentralized: HR is broken up into individual departments, localized worksites, or branches.

- Account Management: Individual HR professionals work closely with individual business units and are accountable to department directors. They have a dotted line to the central HR team.

The services themselves are still delivered primarily in one of four ways. The first – the Generalist approach – is used in multiple models. The others follow Ulrich's "3-legged stool" approach to HR service delivery.

- Generalist: The traditional model centers around the "generalist" being the one-stop-shop for all HR needs. It often creates a "Jack of All Trades, Master of None" syndrome for the HR professional. Still, it is a versatile model that serves many organizations well. This position is used in multiple settings.

- HR Business Partners: Individual HR professionals work closely with business leaders to improve outcomes through human capital solutions. The emphasis is to contribute to business unit plans, implement HR practices, represent centralized HR, and coordinate HR services.

- HR Shared Services: HR delivers centralized, technology-enabled HR service delivery excellence – frequently in an outsourced model. Teams are often assigned to departments or employee groups to manage the day-to-day HR service delivery. The focus of this model is to deliver HR services, managing routine processes effectively and efficiently. Services may be outsourced, HR is seen often as a "back office" function, systems are centralized, and users are required to call in or log in for essential services.

- HR Centers of Expertise: Specific HR experts are assigned as subject matter experts for HR programs, strategies, policies, and solutions. This model created HR frameworks to develop and introduce strategic HR initiatives. It made specialized areas such as compensation, employee relations, learning, and development. It often depends on the business partners to roll out programs to the specific business and units.

HR Isn't Working

Business leaders express frustration with HR failing to meet their needs under the current service delivery model options. When considering workplace demands (both present and future), HR cannot meet the needs of a mobile, remote, and global workforce following the traditional delivery structures. A few of the most commonly mentioned obstacles are described in the following sections.

Lack of Strategic Focus

Even though we talk about strategic partnerships and alignment, the attention of these models still tends to focus on problem orientation and cost reduction rather than strategy enablement. To become a strategic leader,

HR must develop a future orientation. We need to stop focusing on fighting the fires and instead figure out how to prevent them – no, how to grow better forests.

Our business structures support our strategy. If our service delivery model structure is built to mitigate, react, and respond rather than lead, our natural approach will be tactical and reactive. We need a different model to provide an extra level of service to achieve different results.

Poor Execution of HR 2.0

When we evolved the role of Generalist to HR Business Partner, how many of us simply changed the title but kept the same functions in the job description? (Come on, be honest.) The primary purpose of creating the Business Partner model was to become more strategic in executing the HR function. The title sounds better, and it sounds like we should have better access to managers from a trust and credibility standpoint. However, if we didn't change the fundamental nature of the job – for example, we still retained 50% of the position as an administrative processing function – then it did not meet the original objectives.

Additionally, if we created models such as shared services, did having an on-site HR professional help? Or did it just create another layer of HR that employees had to navigate? Did the on-site HR person commonly say, "let me check with headquarters"? Were they continuously aligned with the business? Were they there to meet the needs of the individual business leader – or *only* to ensure that the local business leader was following central HR's policies? You can start to see where the complications set in.

Bad Process

Despite our best effort to automate – if you automate a bad process, it's still a bad process. If we cannot get our transactional house in order, employees remain confused, managers still waste time, and we still spend inordinate amounts of time on things that we should not. As transactional functions continue to absorb our time, we have less to devote to strategic areas. When we are called away to fix transactional problems, executives take note, and they will recognize that we are just too busy to help them out. We become less valuable as a resource.

Competency Challenges

Similar to the change in job title without the change in job functions, did we provide our HR professionals the training and development that they need to be strategic partners? Let me be clear – consulting requires an entirely different skill set than an administrative support professional. Having spent many years doing both, you cannot simply jump over to a manager's office, answer some questions, and call yourself a consultant. It doesn't work that way. However, I have met many HR professionals that have called themselves consultants yet are far from it. They can tell me what the current policies and procedures are. Still, in terms of coming up with creative solutions and strategies related to the business, operations, production, sales, and marketing, they were no help.

We can create the titles, but we cannot simply dream up the competencies. Without developing the competence to support the strategy development and leadership, we remain inept as a solution. While we have touted ourselves as a strategic partner, we have not done ourselves any favors by staying in our HR silo. We become very competent at the HR functions. We are excellent at identifying competencies, describing the hiring process, talking about performance management, termination procedures, and compliance. But are we able to talk strategically about how our specific talent strategies tie into the current demand management load? Can we talk about our time and attendance issues affecting bottlenecks in production, workflow strategies, customer service issues, or sales strategies that we can solve through our employee development programs? Unless we can connect the dots specifically and connect it to the bottom line, managers don't want to hear it. They'll still come to us when they have a problem - but don't expect to have the invitation to the strategy meeting if you don't have anything to contribute actively.

Lack of Personal Touch

Remember what we've said about the focus on employee experience? Regardless of the desire for more automation, people still want a high-touch experience. That doesn't necessarily mean that we need to visit each person daily. However, it does mean that we need to spend more time connecting with the individual. The HR functions that miss the mark tend to try to automate the wrong things.

Emphasizing automation to free up time so you can spend more time on the things that matter most is the correct answer. Automating your way out of touching the employee is the wrong answer.

HR must find opportunities to integrate people and technology to create unique, personalized experiences. The technology exists. The capability and competency are needed to ensure our talent have the experiences they crave.

Failing to Support Your Key Customer

If HR wants to be a strategic partner, it needs to support its primary strategic customer – the manager. HR should spend a disproportionate amount of time investing in developing, assessing, and selecting managers. This is especially the case for line managers as they are typically the entry-level that grow into higher ranks. The more you can invest in them, the greater the ROI as they stay and grow with the company. When HR becomes too busy to develop these developmental support efforts, the company suffers. HR has missed the mark when its service delivery model cannot spend a sizable portion of its time taking care of this constituency.

Failing to Know Your Employees

When HR maintains such a distance that it is unfamiliar with its employees, their needs, attitudes, and wants, they become disconnected. It is through a connection that HR can be effective in understanding and delivering on the employee experience. The experience happens during the recruiting and onboarding phases but must be maintained throughout the entire employment period. Failing to recognize what is essential to employees means that HR cannot design and deliver programs, rewards, and experiences that will continue to meet their needs. This is a recipe for ongoing turnover.

On a global scale, HR must continuously understand its growing population from a cultural and compliance standpoint. HR must become more competent to avoid legal landmines as it operates in other countries and employs individuals in those regions. The complexities of laws in those countries change just as fast as they do in the United States – sometimes quicker. HR can get the company in trouble very quickly if it does not stay on top of it. At the same time, HR must stay on top of cultural norms, connect with individuals within those countries, and stay abreast of changes to be aware of what needs must be met.

What Should Service Delivery Look Like?

There is no "one-size-fits-all" model that works for everyone. Just as a business is only as good as the people that work for it, so too is each organization just as unique. To prescribe a specific delivery model would seem irresponsible given the differences in businesses, types, sizes, challenges, and customers.

What we can do is consider the elements to design the right service model for you. Regardless of your business or structure, the new model must consider the following.

Deliver on EX

Employees need more than just a paycheck from their employment. They crave an experience. In the past, work and life may have been considered separate (though they really weren't). Millennials and Gen Z crushed that perspective as work and life are blended, given that they spend more waking hours with their coworkers than they do their own family. The pandemic exacerbated this symbiotic relationship with the growth in working from home. It also heightened the need for interpersonal relationships, healthcare, mental wellness, and overall well-being. This increased demand for a total employee experience (EX) increases the need to balance work, family, health, well-being, finances, fun, and other aspects of life.

Flexibility

We would like to believe that we are flexible and most of us do a good job. HR must learn to pivot faster and become even more nimble than before. The changes coming our way will continue to increase in frequency and impact. Our focus on compliance with policy and procedure as the basis for business decisions will only hamper the business' ability to react and respond to global demand and prevent it from proactively jumping ahead. HR must increase its capability to adapt faster and farther.

Strategic Orientation

HR must possess the business acumen to provide full-service consultation to leaders throughout the business. They must understand how people affect all aspects of operations, production, sales, customers, etc. HR professionals must add value to helping the company achieve a competitive advantage through its talent management strategy.

Data Analytics

HR needs to turn up the heat when it comes to using data. HR professionals must increase their use of analytics, be skilled in data-driven decision-making, and expand technologies to facilitate their applications.

Do the Basics Better

The essential functions of HR are still needed – paperwork still needs to be done, people still need to be hired, and payroll must be processed. HR needs to find a way to do it better, cheaper, and faster to streamline and automate these functions.

Increase Frontline Support

Remember what we've said – HR is a function, not a department. Our role in the HR department is to help facilitate the execution of HR on the front lines. The better that we can help managers do their jobs, the better we do our job. Next level HR means finding new ways to improve managers' capabilities, talent, and systems to manage their people.

Deliver on ROI

HR needs to join the rest of the executive team and recognize that it must earn its keep. It must shift from its perceived role as an overhead cost to increase its value, decrease its costs, and find ways to demonstrably contribute to the bottom line. It must find a way to deliver value to employees, managers, and the business at all levels.

Shifting Perspectives

The fundamental functions that HR has performed in the past still must be done. For example, the paperwork still needs to be processed. However, it doesn't need to be done the same way - or perhaps we don't need as much of it as we think.

Compliance is another area of HR's traditional focus. It must be managed, and HR will continue to do it. But must it be the underlying emphasis in everything that we do?

What we're talking about is taking a different approach. The optimization of this new model can only be achieved if we shift our perspectives. Remember our discussion about mindset? This is where that shift in mindset must take place before our behavior changes. To put it simply and plainly: This is where we ***get shift done***.

Consider the following shifts that must take place if the new model is going to work.

A New Perspective and Attitude

HR is often seen as the "NO" Department. We are known to tell people why they can't do something or why something won't work. To achieve the next level of service delivery, we need to see the transformation to help the business achieve its strategic purpose. The HR leader must be willing to shift from HR homeostasis – its current state – and make fundamental changes in how things are done. This means shifting how HR is done inside and out, changing the dynamics of HR roles and how HR interacts with the business.

HR Roles and Responsibilities Defined

The HR leader must recognize the desired outcomes, the new dynamics, and the specific changes that must be made in the relationships between members of HR (both internally and externally). This also means that roles and responsibilities must be redefined down to the core. As previously called out, this is not a matter of changing the title and keeping the same duties and responsibilities. We tried that once with the HR Business Partner role. In some cases, it may have worked, but in most cases, it didn't do much. If we want the dynamic results we are looking for, that will call for a dynamic shift in the way we do things. Remember the relationship:

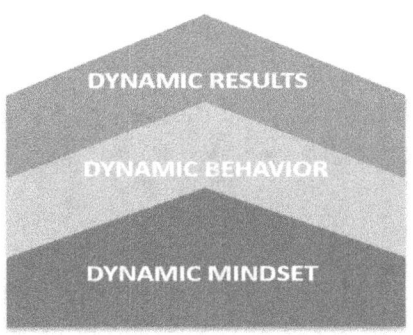

To achieve that level of clarity among your HR team, working on the mindset is critical. However, they also need to know what behaviors are expected to work towards achieving them and attain the desired outcomes. This means the leader must define the specific behaviors from several perspectives.

- Individual: Individual expectations must be laid out. If the individual job description remains the same, but other general behavior changes are expected, they should be clearly defined. If you reinvent the job itself or realign the specific job requirements, those details should be described in a revised job description.

- Team: If the team needs to act differently, be different, or is restructured, this will require clarity. Any time you have different expectations of how the team will collectively behave or perform, this will require a clarification of the shift in expectations.

- Governance: If you are working in a non-centralized format, you'll need to clarify the explicit governance framework of how formal decision-making and HR operations will work under the new model. If there is one group that cannot appear to be working in chaos, it's HR. The leader must define who has responsibility and authority for decision-making as a part of this model.

From Partner to Strategist

The current Business Partner model calls for a generalist who supports the frontline supervisor and employee with day-to-day needs. This is not a partnership. This is a resource. There's no question that the current HRBP model has been helpful in most cases to provide HR expertise to management and employees, but optimization will require more.

Tomorrow's partner will require direct experience in the business itself. These resources will need to bring expertise in the world outside of the HR department to have hands-on exposure to business operations, production, sales, and strategy development. They must have both the acumen and the experience to be equals to senior managers to provide credible consultation in matters that go well beyond operational HR. Instead, these Business Partners can be called upon to:

- Consult on strategy development and implementation.

- Provide professional and career coaching to senior leaders and managers.

- Demonstrate the tangible and business implications of people-related decisions.

- Identify specific business unit requirements to be met by HR programs and staffing.

- Coordinate the best resources and strategies to help business units and their leaders achieve success.

In other words, these Business Partners shift into the role of Business Strategists as they work with managers to align elements of people, practices, and leadership to achieve organizational goals. This multifunctional and interdisciplinary approach requires a new competency base from HR.

Completing the Shift Away from Transactional

In the later stages of HR 2.0, several businesses created operating models charged with setting strategy and delivering solutions focused on helping specific business units or other areas of their organization. Whether using Centers of Excellence (COEs) or some other Shared Services models, most of these projects failed because we just could not get away from our homeostasis. Whether it be pressure from the outside or a default setting on the inside, we just could not get away from the transactional priorities inherent in our nature. We became so busy with the day-to-day that we couldn't focus on what mattered most strategically. As my dad would say, "We major in the minors."

Remember the definition of insanity? If we want different results, we cannot keep doing the same things. We can't become better unless we change – but we have to make the right changes to achieve the right results.

This future-oriented shift still allows us to have a design with COEs or Shared Services built-in. The difference is in how we use them. Anyone familiar with the StrengthsFinder program recognizes the value of identifying our strengths and focusing most of our energy on improving them (versus spending an excessive amount of time trying to overcome our weaknesses). We should recognize our strengths, continue to grow them, and get the people who specialize in those areas to improve them. It's critical that if we do set up these COEs, we do it right. If we do use COEs, it makes sense to consider specific expertise in specialized areas such as:

- **Compliance & Risk**
  Employment law gets trickier with every passing year, and the more countries you operate in, the more complex it becomes. When you add CSR (corporate social responsibility), safety-related risk management (such as worker compensation), and other people-related risks, it makes sense to dedicate expertise to this center.

- **DEI / Employee Engagement**
  While the topic of employee engagement is not new, the issue of inclusion has increased its complexity. Finding new opportunities to engage employees and enhance the employee experience while ensuring diversity,

equity, and inclusion in policies, programs, and activities will remain an essential priority in the future.

- **Data Analytics**
HR is generally perceived as a "soft" area (though most of us would agree that dealing with people is the hardest part of any job in the organization). At the same time, most HR workers are not overly comfortable with statistics, data analytics, and metrics. We can talk about them, but to generate them and integrate them is another story. Working with other managers in the organization to establish KPIs and metrics that will help understand the workforce better is essential – having a team of experts to call upon with this know-how would prove invaluable.

Measuring Your Service Delivery Transformation

As you plan and implement the transformation in your service delivery model, be sure to prepare for your methods to measure and track progress. While the specifics of measurement will depend upon you (what you want, what good looks like, milestones), several scorecards and key performance indicators are commonly used as guidelines. These can help you guide your talent management and human capital strategies, direct the development of your HR programs, and measure your strategic workforce planning effectiveness.

The underlying premise to success when it comes to measures is this:

- That which gets measured gets done.
- That which gets measured and reported improves.
- That which gets measured, reported, and rewarded is repeated.

This is where the value of metrics comes in. If you can define it in measurable terms, people can recognize what you want, how you want it, and how far away they are from it. This is going to take some work, but it will be worth it.

HR Vision

The first step to service delivery transformation is to set a vision of what that delivery model looks like. Set a vision that is:

- Clear and well defined. It should not be so clear that it does not allow for variance, but it should be determined well enough so others can know which direction to take to arrive with you. This is the baseline of the measurability of your service delivery model.

- Brief. The exceptional leader can take a complex concept and break it down into a simple idea. When it comes to your vision, the simpler – the better.

- Abstract and Challenging. The vision should push people, drive them toward the general direction, and challenge them to go further than they would on their own.

- Future Focused. Help others to see beyond tomorrow and picture how things can be if they are successful.

- Desirable. The vision should describe a state that is meaningful and attractive in some way to everyone. You can't please everyone with everything, but you should be able to please everyone with something.

- Aligned. HR exists to facilitate the goals of the company. Be sure that the vision is headed in the same direction as that of the organization.

Business Engagement

Your new business model must be built around full engagement with employees and departments throughout the business. When creating your HR structure, consider whether you are actively strengthening the organization's competencies and its people through the delivery of your services. In other words, do you make the business better by delivering HR? If so, how?

Customer Service

HR must regularly evaluate whether it is serving the needs of its customers – the executives, managers, and employees of the organization. This may require you first to define who your customers are (and in what priority). You may serve multiple masters, and priorities may vary. Clarify your customer and build your delivery model around serving them and meeting their needs.

Programs and Activities

HR must consistently evaluate whether programs, services, activities, and offerings effectively meet the expectations and needs of employees and managers. This will require you to identify the needs, establish your criteria for measurement, execute, and monitor outcomes to evaluate clearly. Be as objective as possible in your criteria for measurement.

HR Proficiency

Consider your efficiency, effectiveness, and timeliness in delivering your promises. Service delivery of the strategic and transactional services must be exceptional. Anything less requires targeted improvement to achieve your standards.

Roles Within Your New Service Model

Your new service model is about evaluating what your organization needs and delivering HR services in a way that meets those needs. This does not mean that we need to come up with new titles. Previous models may work for you – but just in different ways as we apply new methods to meet your changing needs.

I find that when you know what tools are in your toolkit, you can build a better house. Part of the transformation process is to create a better home for the HR function. Let's explore the specific positions available to you and their new roles and tasks after the transformation.

HR Leaders

You can choose your titles, but they will have similar responsibilities. Whether this is your HR Director, VP of HR, Chief People Officer, CHRO, HR Manager, or Head of People, they all share the same governance responsibility.

This group is primarily responsible for engaging with top leaders and representing your organization's HR leadership team. They may engage with the CEO, members of the board, other members of the C-suite, top managers, and essentially anybody in the organization.

This group is still charged with:

- Aligning HR strategy and operations with business objectives.
- Providing strategic direction and leadership for the HR function within the organization.
- Directly leading the HR organization and team.
- Providing governance across HR in the organization.
- Budget oversight and fiscal responsibilities pertaining to HR.
- Direction and allocation of HR resources such as people, money, time.

Business Partners

This group may have several functional titles. Unlike the previous version of the HRBP, this model is not intended to serve as a generalist resource. Instead, this position is meant to provide direct engagement and consultation to key leaders and decision-makers throughout the business.

These individuals are typically integrated throughout the business, working with business units, business partners, and leaders directly or within a Center of Excellence structure.

This group is generally charged with:

- Maintaining top competency levels among HR staff to ensure high-quality delivery of HR expertise to managers and employees.
- Ensure effective HR transactional structures to deliver high-quality functions.
- Deliver strategic support to business units to help meet business goals.
- Provide insights and expertise specific to the people's impact on decision-making.
- Liaise between Centers of Excellence, shared service groups, and managers to deliver required services to business units.
- Demonstrate ROI and value through the delivery of cost-effective HR services.
- Collaborate with business leaders to develop strategies and goals.
- Support business unit strategic initiatives and achievement of objectives.

Centers of Excellence
This model is still available as a viable solution to deliver shared services and collaborative Business Partner resources to business units. Under this model, these Centers...

- Develop specialized expertise in specific areas to serve as content resources to managers and employees throughout the organization.
- Develop, implement, measure, and monitor key HR metrics for reporting purposes.
- Collaborate with shared service centers on complex issues to develop solutions.
- Engage with business leaders and employees on various business problems and opportunities to create optimal programs and outcomes.
- Design standard solutions applicable throughout multiple business units to help align performance directed towards achieving organizational goals.

Development Consultant

This group is dedicated to coaching and mentoring leaders, managers, and employees at all levels and delivering functional HR solutions. This position engages people at the front lines as the incumbents:

- Work with frontline managers to improve HR tools and practices to streamline administrative functions and optimize performance.
- Assess individual competencies and capabilities to identify gaps in required knowledge, skills, and experiences for development.
- Work with managers and individuals to create development plans and implement strategies to prepare future leaders and talent.

Shared Services

As previously described, shared services models provide operational support directly to employees and managers throughout the organization. Specifically, this model is designed to:

- Facilitate transactional functions for employees.
- Manage outsourced services, suppliers, vendors, and contractors.
- Outsource key services (e.g., HRIS/HCM systems maintenance)
- Engage in employee self-service options to reduce administrative burden.

Case Managers

In cases that require extra attention, you may consider a position for handling those complex issues directly. This will help to alleviate the concerns, pressures, and time burdens that take so much time away from the other positions. Whether full-time or part-time (as an assignment and another role), this role can uncomplicate an otherwise active role.

Site Managers

Location-specific HR reps are not a new concept. However, if your organization is at that point where it makes sense to have local HR representation, you will want to ensure they pay attention to local norms, needs, and regulatory requirements. These positions will:

- Maintain compliance with local laws and regulations.
- Establish and maintain relationships with local partners and workforce representatives.
- Deliver support to local sites, especially those with large constituencies.
- Manage site-specific challenges, employee issues, and strategy alignment opportunities.
- Liaise between Central HR and local business operations to ensure consistency.

Digital Transformation

HR Digital transformation is about implementing automation into business processes.

The talk of hiring young and digitally-savvy workers of the future has come to fruition. All employees are digitally engaged in some capacity in their personal lives. Almost everyone uses smartphones, digital media for entertainment, social media for personal engagement, and fully integrated smart platforms in their vehicles. Why should they expect anything less in the workplace?

However, when it comes to HR systems and processes, should it surprise us that as much as 89% of our time is still spent on administrative functions?

Think about it:

- Are most or all your HR systems integrated through a single platform? Or do you still manage your processes through several independent systems? (e.g., ATS is one system, LMS is another system, performance management is another system.)

- How much of your data is tracked on Excel spreadsheets? How much of that data is then input into another system? Do you track it on the spreadsheet because your system is incapable of following it for you?

- Do you find yourself downloading data from one system into an Excel spreadsheet to manipulate it into the correct format so you can upload it into another system?

- Do you still accept paper applications for employment?

- Do you still use paper files for your records?

- How many times do you "touch" a single document?

These are questions that just scratch the surface to demonstrate the need for digital transformation. These transactional processes are essential. I do not question that. What I am asking – and will continue to challenge until I die – is how many steps they require, how much time we spend on them, and why we can't automate them.

The benefits of incorporating digital HR transformation are clear. To name a few of them:

- It saves time. The more time we save by streamlining processes, the more time we have to engage in more meaningful functions.

- It saves money. While the upfront costs are not insignificant, you can run the ROI analysis and easily justify the costs. When you consider the amount of time saved and the human cost of that time, your ROI becomes vividly clear. By shaving off five minutes in one process, that may not appear to be very much. However, if that process is repeated 100 times per year, that is 500 minutes saved. If five people repeat that process, that becomes 2500 minutes or 41.67 hours. That's just over a whole work week saved. Now – repeat that process for the next 5-minutes to be saved.

- It increases satisfaction. As employees can complete several tasks themselves, they can save time contacting or coming to HR. This self-service option is typically favorable due to the time saved, ease of use, and accessibility.

- It increases engagement. Employees appreciate the ability to make their own decisions, make their changes, and engage in the HR adjustments that affect them. The ability to communicate remotely with HR via the web, change their address, make changes to payroll information, access paystubs, process time and attendance remotely, and have web-based services available through their mobile device are all opportunities "touch" the employee.

- We create the workforce of the future. Digital transformation allows for broader reach, a better employee experience, a more imaginative employee exchange, and a more precise level of engagement.

- We increase accuracy in dashboards and data analytics. Better data means better decision-making and better outcomes in our strategy implementation and performance outcomes.

- HR executes workforce management strategies more effectively. We can improve efficiencies as we incorporate artificial intelligence, enhanced reporting, and analytics to meet the increasing business demands.

- Human resources add value to the bottom line of the organization.

Defining Digital Transformation

At a high level, we can define a digital transformation to leverage new, fast, and changing digital technologies to improve the way we do business. If we consider the components of competitive advantage, digital transformation can help us do business better, cheaper, and faster. Enterprises adopt this mindset at every level of the organization, implementing at least one or more technology into their business operations. If they have not done so already, HR must adopt the same mindset to join the business' digital transformation leadership momentum.

Similar to the difference between "change" and "transformation," digital transformation is different from simply upgrading systems to the latest and greatest. Digital transformation requires a different mindset.

Digital change can involve systems upgrades, equipment upgrades, and a new HCM or HRIS system to process and manage data. Those are all cosmetic changes that force behavior variance – employees are then required to use these new systems and the new equipment to do the same old process. However, if the methods don't fundamentally change and/or the mindset and attitudes do not change, things will eventually creep back to the way they were.

We typically include three types of technology when we talk about digital transformation in business.

- **Artificial Intelligence**: This typically includes a range of programs that either automate routine and algorithmic tasks or crunch "big data" for forecasting purposes.

- **Anything as a Service (XaaS)**: This term generally applies to the migration of software and data to the cloud. Moving data and services off-site allows companies greater flexibility to adapt more quickly and with less risk.

- **Robotic Process Automation (RPA)**: This typically refers to methods that allow us to configure robots, software, or other technology to emulate and integrate actions of humans interacting within digital systems to execute a business process.

Other technologies such as blockchain, augmented reality, virtual reality, and the Internet of things (IoT) are other contributors to digital transformation. All of them share the common theme of pushing us to rapidly transform the way we do business.

Let's explore how we can incorporate these processes into the HR function.

HR and Artificial Intelligence

(As we get into the specific technologies, we may appear to be splitting hairs between AI, XaaS, and RPA. These are simply examples of how HR can adopt digital transformation into their strategies to adapt to the HR 3.0 lifestyle.)

When we refer to AI, there is often a misperception that we cannot use it unless we have a technical background or something to be used in the future. It is also seen as something that requires "big data" to be helpful, or it may invoke fear of "Big Brother" dehumanizing operations. Let's get honest about AI. It's here, we're already using it, the majority of employees are optimistic about its use, and we become more efficient with its increased use.

Digital natives make up most of the workplace (Millennials, Gen Z, and whatever comes next). They want a simplified experience with AI for better interfaces, training, and a personalized experience. At the same time, security and privacy are at the top of the list of concerns. AI can help support all of these. Here are a few areas where AI can be used.

HR Reporting
AI redefines the relationships between employees, managers, work, and the environment within which they work. Integrating AI into HR helps businesses to analyze, predict, and diagnose people-related data better and improve decision-making[7]. In a recent study among 8,000+ employees over ten countries, AI is trusted more for accuracy and advice than humans[8]. Implementing AI in automating reporting reduces admin time, increases accuracy, and streamlines HR and managers' processes throughout the business.

Talent Lifecycle: Attracting Talent
Engaging applicants using smart interactive chatbots allows candidates to receive answers to most standard questions through the application process. This will enable employers to free up precious employee time, optimize candidate engagement with real-time interaction, improve response time (candidates don't have to wait for answers on the phone or via email response), and have a more personalized experience.

---

7 Matsa, P. and Gullamajji, K (2019, Aug.) To Study Impact of Artificial Intelligence on Human Resources Management. *International Research Journal of Engineering and Technology, 06:08*, https://www.irjet.net/archives/V6/i8/IRJET-V6I8226.pdf.
8 https://www.oracle.com/corporate/pressrelease/robots-at-work-101519.html

Smart Digital Forms
Applications are tedious when filling out the same information repeatedly. Companies can integrate AI to transfer data from applicants' resumes into smart digital forms and more efficiently complete their applications. This information can also be used to send through background checks and new hire information.

Leverage Transactional Data
AI can leverage workforce data to predict employee performance, potential, fatigue, flight risk, and overall engagement. It can build personalized schedules, as well as review time-off and shift requests based on pre-determined rules. These free up tremendous time for managers and HR as the system can make core decisions for 80% or more of standard functions.

Learning
Most organizations use some form of learning management system (LMS). Delivering videos or some other online content is familiar. The differentiator is whether you allow the learners to determine the direction of their learning and development. As employers integrate AI to recognize employee learning patterns, enable employees to "choose their learning adventure," and uphold quality standards in its content, learning can grow exponentially. Integrating agile learning models supports the employee experience, personalizes the learning journey, matches content based on relevancy, and provides real-time responses to frequently asked questions.

Workforce Analytics
At the core of AI is workforce analytics. AI can automate collecting, analyzing, and reporting critical data for individuals, managers, and groups throughout the organization. Automating analytics and reporting can streamline hundreds of hours and improve accuracy to improve decision-making when it comes to your people.

HR and XaaS

Let's get the terminology straight. This is *anything* as a service. We throw around the term SaaS – Software as a Service. We also use IaaS (Infrastructure as a service), PaaS (Platform as a Service), and everything else as a service. This means that we buy what we need when we need it, how we need it. Uber is a XaaS. You only call upon the service when you need it. It's a cost-effective way to get what you need. The same thing applies to the products and services you need to deliver HR.

HR has been notorious for buying "stuff" and putting it on the shelf – we needed it one time. It cost a lot of money, we used it, and never needed it since. It's time for HR to come up to speed with the rest of the business. We can be more innovative, faster, and more cost-sensitive. It will help us deliver better services more effectively and faster to our people.

HR Legal Services
Many HR professionals turn their attention to multi-employer support groups that offer a subscription-based service to provide employment law advice. Rather than

paying an ongoing retainer fee to a local attorney or paying by the hour, they pay an annual subscription fee to access employment law advice from on-call attorneys.

HCM/HRIS

If you are still using on-premise HR software, it's time to move to the cloud. Traditional on-prem software options had been seen as advantageous due to data controls, security, or fear of downtime. The downside to on-prem services included the need to upgrade (and pay dearly for those upgrades) continuously. Subscription-based cloud SaaS models provide fast, secure, and reliable access that also improves access to your employees to their data. The increased access also increases their ability to engage in self-service activities (thereby reducing their workload for standard requests and form completion functions).

Analytics

HR analytics beg for a XaaS model to allow for continuous updates from third-party software providers that track data, integrate multiple software platforms, report metrics, and populate dashboards. Managing that kind of functionality yourself demands extra staffing. Outsourcing these functions frees you from unnecessary overhead.

A Note on XaaS Partnerships

We have all had great partners and not-so-great partners when it comes to outside vendors. There are few partnerships as critical as your XaaS partnerships – especially for your HCM / ERP. When shopping for a new HCM SaaS model, my goal is to encapsulate as many services as possible under one umbrella. The more services I can shove under one "umbrella," the better. It allows me to manage fewer moving parts. It provides employees a one-stop shop for services, and it increases convenience to save tremendous amounts of time for HR, managers, and employees.

Everyone will tell you that they can improve your efficiencies. ALL of them will tell you that they integrate with any system. Most of them will also tell you that they can equally perform all functions effectively. Let's be honest: no system out there can do everything perfectly. It's still a system and is not perfect. Avoid the oversell.

Here are some tips when shopping for your XaaS partnerships.

- Know what you want. Identify your top goals (in priority order) from your system. Different systems are better at some things than others – knowing your priorities can help with the selection process.
- Recognize your pain points. Identify your top areas that are NOT working or that are problematic. You do not need to identify everything, but at least know your "Top 10" list to see what you need to avoid. These are landmines to avoid in your new partnership.
- Imagine a "best-case scenario" from a new system or solution. This becomes a perfect state. You may find that your ideal option is not possible. That's OK – at least you know what you're aiming for so you can get closer through the process.

- Do your due diligence. When you do your homework, don't succumb to the "wine and dine." All salespeople throw in the flash. Get past the "shine" and get into the systems and functionality.
- If it is a system, ALWAYS invite your IT director to the table. We get sensitive in HR about wanting to maintain the final say in selecting our systems. We often feel that when IT gets involved, they want to take over the process. Get over that and ask for their expertise. It has helped me avoid making terrible mistakes in the past – I would have made a "good" decision, but their advice helped me make a "great" decision.
- Play in the "sandbox" before making the call. Get in to play in the system before buying. If you aren't the technical expert, get the expert in there to play around. If they won't let you get in there to play first because "it's proprietary," RUN!!!! You wouldn't buy a car before test driving it – why would you spend that kind of money on an ERP before test driving?
- Always vet product users. Don't rely only on the references from the company. Find others who are using the product who are NOT on the vendor's list of recommendations. Find out what people think of the product that has nothing to gain from talking about it.

Your XaaS partnerships can be the key to success with your digital transformation. Make sure you take the necessary steps to find the right ones.

We typically use RPA as the driver behind upskilling employees as machinery replaces workers in performing routine tasks. Employees are required to maintain greater proficiency in their knowledge and skill base. This is also the reason we rarely associate RPA with HR. After all, what could we possibly "robotic-ize" in HR? When we break it down to the notion of replacing routine tasks and integrating people with tech, HR can and should lead the way with RPA.

As we implement software robots to perform high-volume, repetitive operational tasks to perform what HR employees currently do, we increase automation, save time, and improve responsiveness for employees and candidates. RPA outcomes are:

- Accurate – Big data means greater opportunity for human error. Implementing technology to reduce the "human touch" in data can increase accuracy and free up staff to work on functions with greater strategic value.

- Reliable – Bots can work behind the scenes 24x7. They don't need breaks, don't call in sick, and constantly deliver results.

- Scalable – Tech is tech. Programs are programs. Large or small, you can ramp up or down your technical applications to adapt to your growth.

- Consistent – The RPA algorithms are predictable. You can schedule outcomes, reports, and deliverables based on processing times you know.

- Flexible – Programming works according to your requests. Provided you can add flexibility. Your programming solutions can create flexible business solutions to match.

We can integrate RPA into onboarding, payroll, benefits, and compliance, to name a few. Driving down costs, saving time, and increasing responsiveness are vital metrics that can take your HR function to a new level. Let's explore a few of these in more detail.

CV Screening
Software robots (bots) can gather information from resumes and applications and compare it against a list of specific job requirements. If you are managing large volumes of positions or candidates, this can streamline the search process. Qualified candidates can be moved along to the next level of consideration, and unqualified candidates can be sent the "no" letter. This is completed effortlessly – all without the hours of HR or management commitment to do the same scan for first-round consideration.

Offer Letter Administration
RPAs can assist with offer letters. As the manager narrows down the candidates within the applicant tracking system (ATS), they can automate sending out the "no" letters with a click of a button. Similarly, they can automate the "yes" letter. When it is sent, the candidate can simply "click yes"

within the email to confirm acceptance which triggers the next steps of the automated process (explained in the following steps). These automated steps create new efficiencies, streamline the hiring process, and shorten your time to hire.

Onboarding
Once an employee accepts the position through the HCM system, the bots can detect which onboarding experience to provide the employee based upon the job. This is automated – enrollment into the onboarding experience, guidance through enrollment into employment processes, and other steps associated with the employee experience. While this is not meant to completely replace all human contact, it can significantly enhance the employee experience.

Data Management
Standardized reports, data feeds, and multiple database management are all good reasons to set up automated bots to manage data flow. Ditching the manual spreadsheets and moving to automated reporting can save collective thousands of hours for your HR and management staff.

Payroll Processing
RPA is perhaps most apparent in payroll with the large amounts of data to collect and process. Connecting multiple systems as you manage time and attendance, HCM/HRIS, and budgets calls for automation. HR has traditionally spent far too much employee time working these systems manually. Integrating RPA to automate these systems is an easy answer.

Expense Management
How many days' worth of time has been spent chasing down a receipt for $10.95? It doesn't make sense. Bringing in RPA to collect, coordinate, process, and manage receipts, expenses, and reimbursements can drive efficiencies and reclaim an incalculable volume of employee hours.

Time and Attendance
Automating time and attendance is an easy answer for RPA. Point of collection options using geo-tracking, cellphone input, biometrics, mag card, and other non-paper solutions for time input to automate time tracking, increase accuracy, and streamline hours of manual labor. Attendance options work the same way with self-service time-off requests, automated reporting for absences, FMLA tracking, and more.

Performance Management
Employers using KPIs and business-generated metrics can integrate business performance reporting into individual performance appraisals and other management systems. RPA allows managers to pull up performance management tools with comparable KPI results at the department or organizational level against which they can measure individual performance.

Background Verification
Third-party integrations become easy with RPAs. With the same click of a button that accepts a job offer, a request can be immediately programmed to send to a third party to

conduct the pre-employment criminal background check. With the outcome parameters pre-determined, the third party can simply report the results and upload them directly to the HR system to let the company know if the candidate is eligible for hire. What took even a few minutes in the past (to set up the background check for a candidate) now takes zero time. When multiplied by the number of new hires per year, those are real dollars saved. This same approach can be used for pre-employment background verification (third-party), drug tests, and other functions.

HR and Other Digital Transformations

Augmented Reality
Augmented reality allows users to merge virtual reality with their environment. Employers can use AR to enhance experiences in areas such as interviewing and training. Several employers have integrated VR goggles to allow candidates to see and interact with virtual interviewers who ask job-related questions. Candidate responses are recorded and evaluated either using AI or a human rater.

Training is another excellent use for AR. In manufacturing, we struggle to find and develop qualified talent. For example, many welding candidates apply with experience, but that experience is often gained on the farm or in the garage. As we work on multi-million-dollar equipment, we require highly skilled fabricators, and that competency comes from education, training, and experience. Our training options had been limited to hands-on "shop time" until we came across virtual welders.

Using AR, welders can use the same equipment as they do in the shop. They interact the same as with real welds, seeing and feeling a simulated experience. In many ways, this becomes a better experience as this solution can provide instruction, visual demonstrations, testing, and test results. This increases efficiency and effectiveness for all parties.

Blockchain
HR must consider new technologies in security due to the need for heightened security. Data related to pay, healthcare, finance, banking, disciplinary records, performance information, or expense reimbursement demand increased sensitivity. Using technologies similar to those that serve as the backbone to blockchain technology can help improve security. Directly speaking to the blockchain, cryptocurrencies are here to stay. Offering crypto solutions as part of your employee investment solutions or even as an option for compensation distribution may not be outside the scope of what will be considered mainstream.

IoT (Internet of Things)
At its core, IoT connects people, machines, and devices via a single network. This allows us to exchange data without manual involvement automatically. It is another way of saying what we've discussed to a degree under XaaS and RPA. Building systems, programs, processes, and solutions with the end-user in mind – AND their access point (knowing that 80%+ of all users will access your systems using a mobile device) – you can begin to understand the importance of HR managing the entire **EX** (*Employee*

Experience) and not just the person. It is the integration, alignment, and connection of computers, phones, tablets, and wearables. It's not enough for them to work independently with your systems. It's a matter of all of them working **together** with your systems.

Pushing HR to Become a Leader in Digital Transformation

Remember the definition of leadership – it's influence. We cannot influence anything in the organization to transform if we are not transforming. It is difficult (if not impossible) to create a massive transformation without the digital systems, infrastructure, and processes to support it. As you walked through the previous list of opportunities to expand your digital footprint, you may have recognized some, most, all, or none of them that you are in the works to adopt. I get it – it's a complicated proposition.

Like any other "transformational" change, it's easy to get caught in analysis paralysis. We look at the entire problem and try to solve the whole thing before working on the first step. In a case such as digital transformation, we may not have the know-how or technology yet to solve our problem. That doesn't mean that you cannot take the first step. Consider the following questions to elevate the conversation with leadership around digital transformation:

How is our operating model changing?

Consider your HR operating model and the changes that you must make to meet the needs of your business. This is largely based upon changes to the industry, customer, production, and other factors in how the company is adjusting to the "new normal" of today's reality. HR must realign its delivery model – and its supporting digital strategy – to match the operating model of the organization. You want to deliver HR where your people are (and in the way they want it).

Does our talent meet our needs?

This is at the heart of everything that we do. As the company pivots to meet changing demands, its strategies must match those shifts as well. This may call for a shift in the competencies required from employees to accomplish those goals. HR must have the processes and systems in place to measure, evaluate, assess, and track talent and how it aligns with company needs.

How will we create consistency?

Within the chaos of an ever-shifting world, HR must maintain a system to consistently align, measure, and ensure stable performance among employees. Long gone are the days when this could be managed by hand. Changes happen too fast and are far too complex to manage by paper. Even if someone electronically tracks it, a different level of sophistication is required that goes well beyond an Excel spreadsheet. HR must pivot to use the tools available to automate its way out of administrative homeostasis and create a better opportunity to manage the workforce. This creates a better experience for the employees and frees up time for HR to focus on new opportunities.

How can we start?

Many change initiatives are hampered simply by delaying or avoiding the start. Once you take that first step, you create the momentum to keep driving forward. You don't need to see the top of the staircase before taking the first step. Finding just one thing to change is good enough – then you can find another thing and so on until you gain momentum with your efforts.

How can we do more of it?

Starting with your "low hanging fruit" helps you get your feet under you when practicing transformation. Creating smaller wins by practicing change in smaller increments is a start, but as soon as you get a few wins under your belt, you need to move on to the next priority. Knowing what is on your "list" can ensure you work on the right changes in the correct order and maintain your momentum in the right direction.

How can we do it faster?

You will become proficient in your digital transformation efforts with practice. Just be sure to run through the entire implementation cycle, including measurement and evaluation, to apply lessons learned.

Improving Process Before Transformation

It is common for leaders to want to jump into the transformation and begin to make the changes right away. Knowing that we must change before improvement comes, many will want to skip to the end to move on to the next adventure. Unfortunately, they miss a crucial component required for effective transformation. Yes – we want to take that *Quantum Leap* into the transformational mindset; however, most structural processes will require a managed approach to navigate the change process.

Let's lay the groundwork by recalling that processes and systems are two separate things. The system automates processes. Systems facilitate the execution of processes. However, systems cannot by themselves improve processes. If we do not take time to improve a bad process, *it's still a bad process.*

As part of *digital transformation,* we must include continuous process improvement (CPI) to prepare for and navigate our change. This will help set up your digital transformation strategy as you recognize the difference between processes, systems, and their interrelationship. (We'll discuss more CPI in our discussion about Change Leadership.)

Taking time to identify and break down your processes is essential before redesigning, purchasing, replacing, or building new systems. Knowing what it is that you are trying to do is critical. The chances are that you have several processes in place with far too many steps (or perhaps the wrong steps). Your system should be there to automate your process – and it will continue to do so, good or bad.

To begin, let us consider a step-by-step approach to identify significant processes and break them down. Within each step, consider how to move closer to optimizing your approach to allow your system to work better.

A Practical Model for Process Improvement

Consider this model when evaluating your processes.

Identify Process
The first step is to identify your processes and break them out into individual steps. This will require you to pull out procedures, write down instructions, and otherwise document your regular activities. As you identify your HR

processes, you may only want to start with a handful at a time to avoid overload. Choose 5-10 to begin.

Suppose you recognize that one or more of these processes is problematic. In that case, you can quickly shift into problem identification – asking (a) *if* you have a problem and, if so, (b) **what** specifically your problem is. The more detail you provide in defining the specific steps, the easier it will be to work through the following stages.

Measure and Assess
With each procedure and process, measure the key performance indicators that impact your people, department, and organization the most. Consider time, money, and overall impact on broad resources. For example, how many steps of approval does it take to hire? What are the steps required by all parties to complete a performance evaluation – and how much time does it take to complete each step (on average)? If a manager wants to hand out a bonus, what is that process? Specifically, the measurables can help with the next steps.

Analyze Efficiency and Effectiveness
The next step is to recognize opportunities for improvement. Considering elements such as problem identification, prioritization (urgency vs. importance), and how deep and wide of an impact the procedures have can help with the analysis. This is part of the initial process to gain an understanding of the current status and measure the gap between where you are and where you want to be.

Consider Optimization
With the gaps in efficiency and effectiveness identified, it's time to consider your options. Creating a strategy or action plan comes next as you direct your efforts to ensure your improvement efforts. Recognizing your problems is not enough – you also need a solid strategy to understand how to achieve your desired outcomes and communicate them clearly to everyone involved.

Implement Solutions
Execution is the key to success. The fifth step to our success model is to get things done. It sounds easy enough, but it is also the top reason for failure in improving. Most managers say they know what needs to be improved, but the difference is found in actually making it happen.

Monitor Controls
Setting clear parameters and guidelines is critical to let leaders and employees know "how we do it around here." These controls establish the rules to work within and boundaries for an order required to create and maintain consistency in your outcomes.

Evaluate and Adjust
Improvement requires a continuous process of assessing progress, adjusting, and moving forward. No change process is perfect, and we all need to be allowed to make mistakes, learn from them, and make the required adjustments to improve as a result.

Standardize

Once we find out what works, it is important to turn those new processes into new habits. This standardization process does not happen naturally. With guidance and a few steps, managers can build new behaviors into the culture.

Lather – Rinse – Repeat

It's easy for us to want to take on everything when it comes to process improvement. Attempting to go from "here" to "there" in one fell swoop is the temptation, and when we try, we become overwhelmed and quit.

Begin with your "Top 10" list prioritized according to urgency, importance, or even ease of completion for your first try. Run through the cycle with a handful of processes to learn the model, apply it successfully, and tailor it to your team. As you become comfortable with the flow, go to the next group of processes and do it again.

As you build a culture of the continuous process into your team, you will notice ongoing improvements in multiple areas that emerge (and not just in the targeted regions). It will create momentum that drives a culture of improvement and help maintain process improvement as you work through digital transformation and other shifts during your journey.

People Transformation

It was a typical day on my first job when Mike – my first boss and mentor – stopped in while I was working. He was always good for a story, a soundbite, and a word of wisdom that I would never fully appreciate until years later. I reflected on this very day shortly after I heard of Mike's passing a few years ago because of its impact on my life journey. He told me, "Wade – remember that you can do things for employees that they cannot do for themselves. Always try to do better for them. They're counting on you!"

That has stuck with me for years. In our role in HR, we can facilitate opportunities for employees that they may not have access to. We can influence their employment, hiring, onboarding, compensation, benefits, wellness, and so much more. These are programmatic parts of employment that can significantly impact employees and their families.

HR must become more proficient at enhancing the employee experience and delivering on our promise. Our success as a business depends upon our ability to deliver on our commitment to the customer. We rely on our employees to make that delivery. The better the partnership we can build to create an environment conducive to happy, productive employees, the better our ability to achieve business results. You see – people aren't crucial to our business. People *are* the business.

People must also be at the heart of the transformation process. As HR builds its strategy to create the desired outcome, it must remember the primary reason behind the move. Your efforts will be limited if you only focus on process improvement as the primary motive. Instead, we must recognize that our goal is to transform the hearts and minds of our employees to perform differently to achieve this transformation and achieve a higher level of performance.

People are the means through which you can accomplish the broad transformation of HR. It is through their experience, development, and growth that you can achieve your change.

Foundational Principles of People Transformation

Everyone seems to want to improve, but no one wants to go through the requisite change to get there. Nobody likes to change _unless_ it's their idea. So how can we energize the workforce in a way that makes them want to engage in the transformation process? How can we create the context to help them see change as something they want to help make? Consider some of these ideas.

Focus on Clear Business Outcomes

Before you can ask people to change, they will want to know *why* they should change. The primary question is: **What's in it for me?**

We are all incentive-based: the bigger the change and the greater the transformation, the more significant the impact on the individual. Simply asking them to change and trust in you is not enough. They need to know where you are headed and why it matters to them. What is the inherent reward for helping you get there? Talking about greater efficiencies, effectiveness, and metrics are nice – but unless they are directly impactful to the individual in a way that helps *their* lives to be better, easier, and more profitable, it's not enough to motivate individual commitment.

The outcome must be clear about what you expect from your transformation initiative and its role in the process. Identify one or two priorities, keep it simple and focused, and define how you want the workforce to change. By setting clear expectations, individuals affected by the change can know the anticipated level of transformation and what you are asking of them. You can't get what you don't ask for, and they can't fix what they don't know. Don't be afraid to ask specifically and directly.

Win Their Hearts

To make transformation successful and lasting, you will need more than simple behavior change. Creating simple incentive-based behavior changes will not be enough to drive lasting significant change. You will need to connect with their emotions to help link them to a larger purpose and develop a passion for the transformation outcomes.

Many leaders avoid connecting emotionally because it may feel too "touchy-feely." We like to remain objective and avoid feelings. We are all emotional creatures – there is no way to separate emotions from people. There is nothing wrong with discussing feelings. It's not a bad thing. Understanding those feelings and helping employees connect them to a central purpose can be to our benefit as they become emotionally committed to the transformation.

Your behaviors as a leader are important. Others will queue off your comments, behaviors, and observable responses. If your excitement is visible, you articulate energy, you "walk the talk," and your enthusiasm is contagious. This emotional projection catches on and inspires others to commit.

Consider the user experience (UX) in programming design. We are concerned about how the user engages and feels about their experience with an app, program, or overall engagement with software or hardware. Let's apply the same concept with the employment experience and use the same level of concern for our new employees and how they perceive the employee experience (EX). Do you apply the same standards and level of scrutiny for EX with your employees as you do for UX with your customers?

Consider what EX involves. It begins before employment with the initial application process. The individual is influenced by their interaction with your advertisements, applicant tracking system, and interaction with your recruiters and HR. From there, the hiring process, onboarding process, and new employee experience all lay the foundation for first impressions and initial attitudes for the employee. In many cases, this is where the focus on EX ends. However, the employee is still there. We must not forget continuing elements of their employment such as performance management, corporate communications, coaching, mentoring, compensation, rewards, recognition, professional development, activities, and much more.

The quality of the employment experience affects morale, productivity, and performance while the employee is there. It impacts others negatively when a disgruntled employee affects their workflow due to poor quality, missed deadlines, or customer complaints. Alternatively, a good employee experience can positively impact the individual and their coworkers as they support high morale, higher productivity, higher quality, and higher levels of performance.

Invest in People

Transformation is a significant investment, and most employees will benefit from it. However, some individuals' roles and talents will be critical through the change process to achieve your goals. It is essential that you maintain and increase your investment in people to optimize your ability to tap into those talents during the transformation process.

The process of "upskilling" is essential to your ongoing success through the transformation process and beyond. The standard rate of change for any organization creates obsolescence of knowledge and skills over time. Transformation increases the rate of obsolescence exponentially, thereby requiring a heightened effort before, during, and after the process to continuously enhance professional growth.

We will discuss the role of upskilling shortly. The transformational HR leader must build continuous upskilling into the culture to ensure ongoing continuous improvement in the workforce's knowledge, skills, and capabilities. Your business' continued competitive advantage depends on it.

Start with Behavior

The transformation will ultimately change both the behaviors and mindset moving forward. Changing mindsets takes time, but we can begin to change behaviors right away. Explicitly designing and instilling new approaches can engage new critical behaviors that we want to see throughout the business or within a specific function. These can translate into day-to-day actions and include clear behavioral expectations for employees. They are further engrained into performance expectations and accountability measures (e.g., coaching, counseling, performance evaluations, rewards mechanisms).

Ongoing training, development, and repetition of these behaviors are critical to enhancing knowledge and skill. Some new behaviors require considerable time to master due to their technical complexity, scope, or depth of knowledge or skill. This learning can only come from doing. Part of the transformational process must include consideration for learning and development and performance accountability to ensure ongoing upskilling and reinforcement of the new behaviors.

Promote Innovation

When we talk about change, the difference between the "program of the month" efforts and ongoing initiatives is influenced by sponsorship and buy-in. Top-down initiatives rarely have the buy-in to retain their energy and commitment for long. On the other hand, initiatives generated and implemented at the frontline typically have a better chance because they are solutions that were designed for them and by them.

Effective transformation efforts recognize that the leader does not have all the answers. They are the facilitator to find the answer rather than the provider of all solutions. Inspiring innovation at the front lines creates better decision-making, problem-solving, and commitment. Employees generate their ideas and create their solutions to drive the momentum of the transformation.

A culture of innovation does not happen overnight, but the decision to shift into a culture of innovation can be made immediately. It begins with new mindsets such as:

- It's not "if," but "how." Employees often believe that they can offer an answer of "no" when presented with a challenge – that something is not possible. The influential leaders clarify that the options are not whether or not something is possible but *how* it can be done. The overquoted NASA Apollo 13 mission quote that "Failure is not an option" resonates with innovation.

- The answer always lies within the team. When I attended an executive leadership course at Yale, Ret. Col. Pilar Ryan shared her experiences. As the former commander of the largest artillery battery in the U.S. Army, she shared principles of leadership she had learned from the battlefield. She provided us with context about problem-solving – that there was no problem that she had ever come across that could not be solved by involving the entire team. By bringing everyone together, working collaboratively, and solving the problem together, you could develop better solutions and outcomes. I have found this to be true in every case. You know what to do already. It's a matter of pooling your resources to figure it out.

- Better, Cheaper, Faster. Michael Porter summarized the core principles of competitive advantage in his book Competitive Strategy.[9] These applied before his book and still apply today. The core of innovation is to create a competitive advantage centered around making products and services better, cheaper, and/or faster. We must incorporate one or more of these elements in our internal support practices to achieve our business goals.

Include Everyone EXCEPT the Unwilling

Let's be honest. Not everyone will be excited about the transformation, and there will always be a group of resisters. Your ROI will come from the groups that will evangelize the change, drive it, and support it. Wasting your time on the resisters is just that – a waste of time. They typically represent about a quarter of your group (the true resistors). Avoid wasting any more time on them and let's move forward with your fully engaged team.

---

9 Porter, M. (1998). Competitive Strategy: Techniques for Analyzing Industries and Competitors. Free Press.

Find opportunities to collaborate and involve them in the transformation process. Invite them to focus groups, committees, and other sessions to seek their input. Allow them to provide direct feedback, ideas, and recommendations. At the same time, engage in two-way dialogue with them and communicate openly about progress during the transformation process. Avoid worrying about the 25% that will never come along. Focus on the 75% who are either fully committed or at least agreeable to your goals and generate more momentum.

Preparing to Upskill

Transforming your people will require them to shift from where they are today to where you need them to be. This is presumably a vertical move upward – to take them to a higher level of performance and capability. Many so-called change initiatives fail because they create change but primarily create horizontal shifting that generates disruption but results in little or no progress. Fundamental transformation requires the growth and advancement of the people along with the organization.

Elements of Performance

The vertical movement focuses on performance. To improve performance, let's consider what goes into performance. We recognize that the value of people comes from not only what they bring but also what they can do for us. Consider what they bring – knowledge, skills, education, experience, capability, ingenuity, and performance. Ideally, we can merge all these elements in a way that aligns and generates the highest output possible to benefit productivity. Many managers believe performance is a simple cumulative equation where one plus one equals two.

Knowledge + Skills + Education + Experience = Performance

It does not work that way. We are dealing with humans. People are emotional creatures, and we have variables such as attitudes, health, relationships, distractions, and more that get in the way. We find that these variables interrelate – one factor can have a disproportionate impact on the other. At times, they can impact one another randomly and unpredictably. It creates more of a calculus equation that was best presented to me years ago as:

Performance = f (Knowledge, Skills, Attitudes)

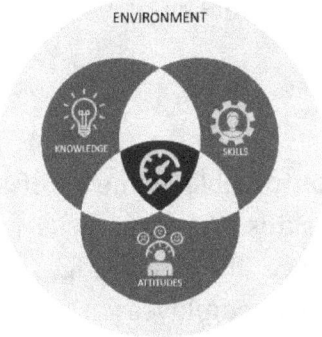

As one person explained it to me after I shared this: "So, what you're saying is that a person typically doesn't perform because they don't know how to perform, are unable to, or don't want to." Thanks for the simplification.

I've also come to recognize the influence of the environment on performance. While some independent will say that it doesn't matter what others think, there is no doubt that the environment in which we live and work has a distinct impact on how we behave and perform.

The essential elements of talent management can be simplified into these primary areas for your employees. Acquiring, aligning, managing, and retaining the knowledge, skills, and attitudes that it takes to do what needs to be done to meet the goals of your business is what the people component is all about. The business' performance is the result of the collective performance of your employees (remember: your organization is only as good as the people that work for it). If you want to increase business performance, you must improve the collective performance of individual employees.

Upskilling Challenges

The two most controllable elements of this equation are knowledge and skills. We can focus on the upskilling process to enhance the knowledge and skills of our workforce to increase employee performance. We find that as people feel better about their capabilities and find success in their performance, their attitudes and morale tend to increase.

While it sounds simple enough – train people and get better performance – there are common challenges when attempting to upskill your workforce.

- *It realizes an ROI from your upskilling efforts.* This takes two forms: timing and measurability.

When it comes to timing, your boss (especially the CFO) wants an immediate return on investment on anything people-related. That's just not going to happen. We cannot invest today and expect to make it back with dividends in 30-days even though we feel that pressure, the same people who are applying the force do not expect the same ROI in any of their other investments. For some reason, executives are OK with ROIs that take years in financial and capital assets but are impatient when it comes to investments in people.

Part of the ROI challenge (maybe most of it) is self-induced as we do not put into place well-defined measurables for progress. Unless we specifically identify how we plan to measure progress and returns, it will be difficult to demonstrate outcomes. Setting your measurables beforehand, working with your employee as a partner to achieve those progress outcomes, and recognizing how to report the ROI metrics can help you achieve desired outcomes more effectively.

- *You are providing employees with the skills necessary to compete.* We may train and develop our employees, but are we putting the wrong tools in their toolkit? Many training programs have not been updated in years. When it comes to external training, do you send your employees to the same course as you always have without evaluating whether their curriculum meets your production needs? Have you re-evaluated the core competencies for key positions lately and compared them against your training requirements? You may be delivering sub-optimal development if it is misaligned.

- *You are revitalizing a disaffected, disengaged employee culture.* If the overall culture is suffering from low energy, low engagement, and low morale, you may face some initial challenges launching an initiative to upskill the workforce. It is not impossible – it just requires a few extra steps to identify the specific needs, create a coalition of supporters, and promote the efforts from within the ranks. Cultural disengagement generally does not happen as a top-down program, so neither will cultural re-engagement. Creating a program that can start small with a handful of groups, finding success, and letting the word-of-mouth approach spread the word, you can create significant momentum to launch a new culture.

- *You are motivating the workforce while transforming.* When you try to encourage <u>after</u> you begin the transformation, it can feel forced. The ideal situation is to generate motivation at least a short time before the transformation efforts. However, events that may not allow for a preparatory period and changes may have to begin immediately. These sudden changes can create massive disruption and resulting distrust. Helping employees work through their frustrations, connect to the transformation in motion, and find their personal role in transformation success can help them find their new roles and create a new commitment.

Strategic Workforce Planning

Recognizing that people are the business and knowing that we need to upskill our employees to meet current and future business needs, the next question becomes – what are our business needs?

We typically break business needs down into two parts: operational needs and people needs.

Operational needs such as finances, inventory, sales, revenue, production, assets, and operations are covered in a company's strategic plan (SP). While people resources are still a significant part of strategic plans, the primary focus of the SP is to take a holistic approach to guide the organization's tangible assets.

People deserve a plan of their own. This plan deserves the same level of attention as your strategic plan because it is effectively the strategic plan to source your people.

Strategic workforce planning (SWP) is not a new concept. It has been around for decades in one form or another. Our approach to SWP has changed considerably, especially in our application to the organization, level of sophistication, and how it is applied.

At its roots, SWP is a structural framework to evaluate the current and future state of the workforce. We compare where we are to where we need to be (or where we want to be). If done right, we can identify what we need to do today to get to where we want to be tomorrow. We can identify areas for improvement, areas for growth, and the steps necessary to get to that desired future.

Businesses develop strategic plans to identify mission, vision, values, and goals. These set the course, energy, and priorities for a company. It defines what, when, how, why, and who will help the company achieve its success. The company gets from its current state to its future state in its overall profitability, operations, and outcomes.

Likewise, the SWP identifies the people, practices, and leadership competencies required to facilitate the strategic plan. It defines the people resources necessary to execute the strategic plan. The SWP runs tandem with the strategic plan through its people as we align skills, programs, teams, and day-to-day work with organizational goals, objectives, and strategies. Understanding what goes into the SWP process will help us better create and manage a strategy to develop the right actions to transform our business.

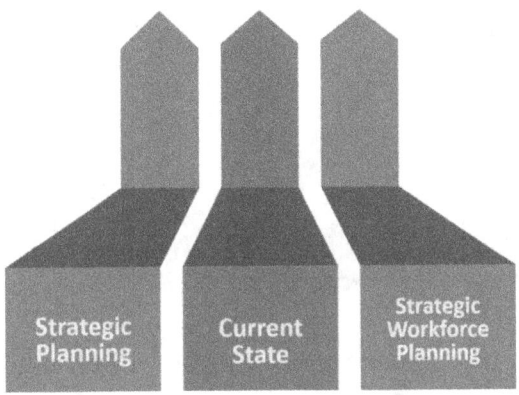

Some may think that this sounds a lot like what you do already. You may track attendance, watch your daily budgets, schedule, create rosters, and manage recruitment plans. While these are forms of workforce planning, they do not arrive at the strategic level.

Consider the following model.

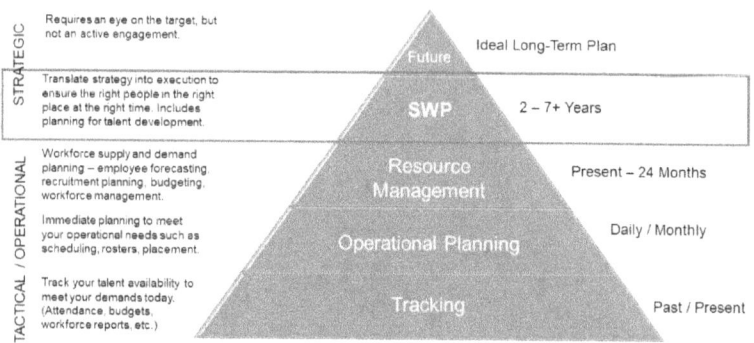

Most of us manage and execute different types of workforce planning. We often manage the day-to-day elements OK – or at least enough to get by. We ensure that we have sufficient people in place to meet the needs of our business. As we track labor, manage reports, work with time and attendance, and otherwise manage our resources, this is indeed a type of workforce planning. The strategic part is looking ahead systematically in a coordinated effort to align people with business strategy.

I recall my first crash course in SWP when I started my career in HR in the fire service. I worked for a special district in the Portland metro area. Based on the retirement system, we could predict almost to the day when someone would retire. Given the nature of how we grew the organization by acquiring smaller departments to streamline operations for surrounding cities, we were a mix of several employees who had been hired over many years. Curious to know simply what the retirement projection looked like for purposes of recruitment, leadership growth, and skills development, I ran a tenure analysis for the workforce. I had to run it three times because I couldn't accept the results the first two times – or I didn't want to believe them.

My analysis discovered that nearly half of my emergency services crew would retire over the next five years. I slipped into a panic. Why? Let's consider who would retire – captains, lieutenants, apparatus operators, senior firefighters, and experienced paramedics. At a minimum, it takes ten years to train up a captain. If someone is on top of it, we could get someone to lieutenant in five years. The other positions are skilled and require years of training, aptitude, and experience to get no other way except to be on the job. You can't "cram" this kind of experience. Let's be honest – if you were the one who needed the first response, do you want the person who has a few months on the job? Or who has a few years under their belt?

This kind of scenario changes your perspective on hiring. We were no longer hiring baseline firefighters. Sure, we need good technicians. At the same time, we are looking for additional competencies that go beyond firefighting. We were looking for people who could grow, develop, and lead. We are looking for future leaders, fast learners, and collaborators who can move them and their team forward. It's no longer a search for the best individual, but instead, it becomes a search for the best component to a complex system upon which the entire organization depends.

Since this experience, I have discovered through the past couple of decades:

- We all must undertake this level of analysis for our workforce. It may not be a matter of preparing for retirement but knowing our risk of turnover at any given time is essential.

- Recognizing our desired future state makes it easier to identify what talents we need today from our employees to help us get there. Whether it comes from new hires or current employees, knowing what knowledge, skills, and capabilities it will take to get from here to there will help us to go looking for them in our people.

- Our ability to identify, measure, and assess talent in our employees is essential. Once we understand what we need (our desired future state), we can better identify those competencies required for success in the position, develop methods to measure individual strengths within those competencies, and assess employee performance to deliver within those competencies.

- As we improve our ability to match individuals with the correct positions, our organization will expedite our journey to the desired end state. Helping to identify and hire the right talent is excellent, providing solid direction is better, and then delivering top talent management solutions to help them succeed is best.

The Basics of SWP

A manager recently asked me, "Isn't workforce planning just a new name for succession planning?" I had to respect his candor – we are often accused of changing the name and selling the same product package in HR. I respectfully offered that succession planning could be included as an SWP, but SWP was not succession planning. Here are the key differences:

- Succession planning is typically managed as a mitigation tool. It tends to focus on what happens when vacancies occur and how to fill in the holes when they happen. The primary emphasis of succession planning is often to identify what competencies are *currently* required for critical positions, evaluate the *current* talent, measure the gap, and strategically develop individuals to fill those gaps in preparation to fill future vacancies.

- Strategic workforce planning recognizes the current scenarios and builds in strategic flexibility for growth, retention, and resilience. It assesses existing skillsets and considers multiple outcomes for individuals to develop new knowledge, skills, and capabilities. SWP recognizes the ability for cross-training and collaboration throughout the organization and the ability to share resources to optimize performance, develop individuals, and reduce costs. SWP focuses on how to prepare to fill future gaps and seeks to maximize resources to achieve the organization's best performance today.

The following are three essential parts to a strategic workforce plan.

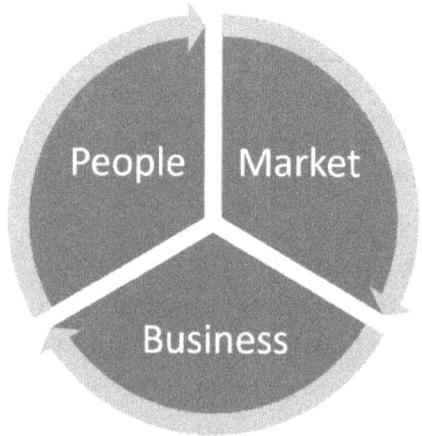

Market
The supply and demand of labor define the market. It can be industry-oriented, position-specific, and talent-driven. HR transformation must take a different approach than simply manage to the market. This is how most organizations work their workforce plans – which is why they don't have a plan at all. Instead, they are influenced and held hostage by the whims and storms of the workforce.

Take just one example where employers took the "market chase" approach. The 2020 pandemic taught us that market trends could be unreliable when it comes to predictions. In that situation, we can simultaneously have unprecedentedly high unemployment and labor shortages. Depending upon the industry, positions, required talents, etc., employers faced significant challenges finding not just people but also the right people, at the right places, at the right times.

In some positions, we had capable workers who were unwilling to work. We also had capable workers who were willing but unable to work due to lack of available childcare, school closures, and health concerns. When coupled with subsidies and incentives to stay home (e.g., enhanced unemployment compensation), employers could not find *willing* workers to fill critical needs. The supply of capable workers was high – people with the right skills and capabilities were available based upon local market unemployment rates – but employers were still unable to find sufficient workers who were willing to come to work for less than what they could make by staying home and receiving unemployment benefits.

In other cases, the pandemic exacerbated an already critically low supply of key talent. Individuals who were on the verge of retirement used the pandemic as the reason to retire early. This put employers in a bind as their available labor in these key talent positions shrank faster than they had anticipated. The market availability to replace those positions also shrank due to the complications brought on by the pandemic. With fewer people in the workplace and a resulting impact on enrollments in higher education, the rate of newly trained employees in these skilled positions created a new lag in an already tight labor supply chain.

While HR should be sensitive to the market and aware of what is going on, it must take a leadership approach to drive the marketplace. Understanding what attracts talent is essential to become the leader in attracting, motivating, and retaining key talent. If we are constantly chasing the market, pivoting to the next benefit or move that behemoths like Google or Amazon offered to their employees, or worrying about what the employer down the street is doing, it will drive us crazy. Rare is the team who can win the game by focusing entirely on defense. HR must shift into an offensive strategy and dictate the terms and conditions of how to attract employees.

Business
Your business strategy should define your business talent needs. While it's true that your business is only as good as the people who work for you, it's also true that the type of people that work for you depends upon what you need. Your business should guide the type of people that you hire. While that sounds obvious, most employers and managers do not hire strategically following that approach.

The corporate strategy consists of the activities, policies, and decisions that an organization utilizes to increase its shareholder value. Regardless of the nature of the business (for-profit, not-for-profit, or government), every organization must define its clear strategy to deliver value to its primary stakeholders, whether they be owners, constituents, or public members. A clear plan consists of "pillars" that set the tone for how the organization creates long-term value. This includes long-term direction, the scope of activities to pursue, its competitive position, its position within the industry, and its culture.

Without a clear direction and strategy, it's difficult to understand the specific competencies and capabilities needed in your workforce. Just as a carpenter needs a set of blueprints for a house to determine the types of materials and tools they need to build it, HR needs a good strategic plan to recognize the nature of talent needed to build and develop a successful business from within. The tools and resources come from the people that work for the business. This includes the people that HR brings in and how current employees are developed, and their performance is managed.

HR must step up to ensure that the business has a clear strategy. If not, it needs to take a more active role in working with the CEO to create that strategy. In the past, HR may have been invited to participate in the strategic planning process. In this transformational role, HR must step up become the major influencer to help develop the company's strategy. When considering elements such as long-term goal setting, cultural development, talent management, and business relationships, these are all in HR's bailiwick.

People
The third element is talent management. We tend to use that term like we have a common definition. Sure – we can consider it strictly from a supply and demand perspective of resource availability. However, people are not like any other resource. We may call them "human resources," but they are far from any other tangible assets.

I previously introduced the elements of performance and its impact on overall business performance. The essential aspects of talent management can be simplified into these primary areas for your employees. Acquiring, aligning, managing, and retaining the knowledge, skills, and attitudes that it takes to do what needs to be done to meet the goals of your business is what the people component is all about.

Typical Workforce Planning

Workforce Planning: Bringing in Workforce Analytics

There is no single best approach to SWP. There are principles to SWP that are essential to its success (and some things that will guarantee disaster). Incorporating a data-driven approach to workforce planning can help ensure an efficient and effective methodology as you achieve your goals.

Remember our basic premises when it comes to measurement:

a) That which gets measured gets done.
b) That which gets measured and reported improves.
c) That which gets measured, reported, and rewarded is repeated.

In SWP, if you don't have specific measures, you have no plan. Data-driven decisions require data – which means we need to bring in the analytics. Accurate data allows us to benchmark, identify trends, understand relationships, recognize gaps, and predict the future more accurately.

The goal of workforce analytics is to obtain insights and predictions that can be used to plan for and improve organizational performance. By combining data specific to employee demographics (information *about* the employees), the employee experience (EX), and the overall impact on the organization (as demonstrated through outcome data), we can start to see how it matters. Pulling data from only one source might be interesting – but it won't tell the whole story.

In one example, an employee engagement survey (information about the employee experience – EX) might reveal that female managers are feeling overworked. By itself, the data may not show anything. However, when correlated with data obtained from consumers (outcome data), we may find a correlation between the female managers who are overworked and resulting disgruntled consumers. Only by combining correlating data from these sources can we identify trends that matter most to the business to provide resources that will alleviate workforce stress, improve customer experience, and retain employees and profits they may have lost.

Examples of Metrics

Analytics may be applied in the SWP process as in the following examples:

Talent Acquisition
You can use SWP data to identify current and future recruitment and staffing needs, trends, and outcomes. SWP can help identify specific competencies, workforce demands, and other criteria to help with candidate selection and process automation.

- Candidate demographic statistics to measure, track, and understand recruitment and hiring diversity trends.
- Time-to-hire information can help to improve the hiring process by streamlining application forms and making it easier for candidates to apply.
- Employment test and interview results can be analyzed for trends, bias identification, and process efficiencies.
- Post-interview surveys can be collected to improve the candidate experience.
- Save time and resources through automation of early-stage candidate screening processes.
- Analytics review from interviews to rule out poor candidate matches.
- Capitalize on key data indicators to readily identify relevant candidates from applicant pools.

Onboarding

SWP can capture critical data during the onboarding process that will be useful throughout employment to align people, resources, and projects. It can also help to automate the employee experience and ensure the best outcomes for both you as the employer and them as the employee.

- Data analytics can capture demographic information about the new hire employee population – who made it through the hiring process and the success factors of those candidates. You can adjust your recruitment and interview practices accordingly to meet goals associated with recruitment strategies, DEI, and other priorities.
- Identify employee experience data specific to perceptions, attitudes, and beliefs to adjust onboarding outcomes continuously.
- Compare results against desired outcome data tracked by the organization, such as attrition, production metrics, or other operational data to identify trends.
- Incorporate surveys to measure the satisfaction of new hires.
- Use testing to measure the effectiveness of new hire learning to increase new hire proficiency and reduce time-to-proficiency.
- Change from "time to hire" to "time to proficiency" as a measure of talent effectiveness.

Talent Retention
HR can incorporate SWP into its retention efforts. It gains a better understanding of employee competencies and needs, current and future business needs, and influential trends from both inside and outside of the organization.

- Employee engagement survey data can be used as a comprehensive measure of employee attitudes and opinions to guide decisions around hiring, benefits, compensation, and more.
- Incorporating micro "check-in" surveys to ask a few questions on a specific topic can engage employees, assess sentiment, and allow businesses to course-correct as needed.
- Track long-term and short-term employee retention in positions and the company, recognizing and correlating relationships and trends.
- Evaluate social "chatter" to determine employee attitudes, preferences, and awareness.
- Assess employee healthcare trends and benefits utilization to identify opportunities for program enhancements or cost savings.

Performance Management
Connecting the right people with the correct positions is the goal of SWP. When talent aligns with opportunity and motivation, high-performance results. SWP can help identify, develop, and track employee competencies; align talent with the right opportunities; navigate succession planning; and manage performance through practical goals and incentives. SWP can integrate processes with systems to optimize talent management to ensure the right

people are in the right places to achieve their best for themselves and the organization.

- Analyze specific performance data, comparing goals to actual performance outcomes, and reporting results accurately and efficiently in real-time.
- Use data from top-performing teams and individuals to understand effective processes and set benchmarks for others.
- Evaluate trends and measure for bias in performance ratings and feedback to reduce negative impacts, promote inclusiveness, optimize outcomes, and ensure compliance.
- Forecast future performance with predictive analytics.
- Track performance evaluation completion to ensure engagement between managers and employees.
- Measure both value and weight of performance metrics to promote desired outcomes.

Project Management
In a typical project, the manager identifies the project needs, considers the required skillsets for their team members, and then looks for the necessary talent. SWP can provide those resources immediately in the PM's hands with the right system to track internal competencies, individual capabilities, and talents and match them through a systematic search process. Consider these benefits of an effective SWP program.

- Competency identification of individuals as you identify, categorize, and catalog (tag) essential knowledge, skills, and abilities held by each employee.

- Identify core competencies required for every position that help to identify talent groups readily.
- Facilitation for PMs to match talent to project competency needs.
- Ease of tracking total competencies within the organization by person and position.
- Gap identification – to more quickly identify those project areas which must be outsourced.

Professional Development

SWP can also be used to identify gaps between what is needed and what exists among your talent and competencies.

- Recognize gaps and areas of development for future workforce needs by identifying required competencies and evaluating against current talent review outcomes.
- Maintain "real-time" succession planning based on turnover projection and needs.
- Provide digital tools for employees to increase value and track the progress of professional development efforts.

Getting Started with SWP

I am a believer in the power of hope. However, I do not believe that hope should be your strategy as a long-term solution. Failing to plan is planning to fail – it's true with workforce planning.

To create a workforce plan that works, you must first understand your workforce. This means more than simply going around to shake everyone's hand. While necessary, that cannot provide the information you need to optimize their performance or the company's outcomes. It takes a coordinated effort to know your resources and what they have to offer. With this information, you can put the pieces in place to enhance your people, operations, and business outcomes.

SWP requires a realignment of your processes and systems to achieve your best outcomes. The previous step of digital transformation applies as we seek to align the strategy with methods to optimize results.

Consider these five steps to align your SWP process and related systems to optimize outcomes.

Define What You Want to Measure

Under our rule of *"That which gets measured, gets done,"* we can apply metrics as those key performance indicators we target within our planning process.

When establishing metrics, remember that not all metrics are created equal. As you consider the laundry list of what you can measure, you will prioritize settling in on a reasonable and workable approach. Everything will seem like the most important thing to be done at the moment. If you can break the priorities down by the categories "urgent" and "important," it may help identify what to work on first.

Below is a chart depicting the 4-quadrants referred to by Dr. Stephen Covey[i]. Applied to SWP measures, we recognize that we cannot and should not measure everything.

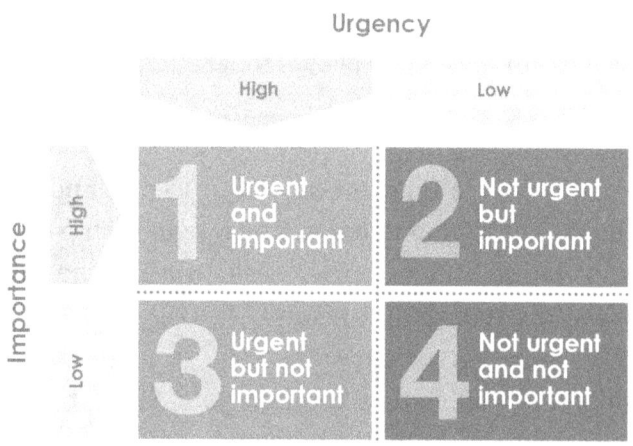

Quadrant 1: Urgent and Important
This is where HR loves to exist. The world is on fire! If you have immediate SWP metrics in this category, they are a MUST to measure. For example, if you have impending vacancies in critical positions or skill gaps affecting your company's ability to compete, these are Q1 considerations.

Quadrant 2: Not Urgent, but Important
This is the strategic and leadership-oriented quadrant. Most things in this quadrant appear at the onset as "nice to do" and expendable. However, the ROI of these tasks is exponentially more valuable than Q1 over time. Am I recommending that you completely forget about Q1 and only do Q2? No. Of course not, but if the shift is going to happen, it starts by aligning your focus on where you want to go.

Long-term development of skills, competencies, and leadership falls into this category. Identifying and developing talent in core competencies, trades, cross-training roles, and promotional opportunities are also here. This creates your ongoing talent pool from which you can draw in the future.

Quadrant 3: Urgent, but Not Important
These are distractors. They appear to be value-adding activities, but in the end, do little (or nothing) to contribute to the result. Identifying these activities can help you avoid them.

In the world of SWP, measuring hours of training by itself is not the right measure. Sending the wrong employees to the incorrect training (e.g., wrong skill sets, wrong competency match) may appear to be a good thing by offering professional development to everyone. However, you will have much better use of time, money, and resources by sending those employees to training to help them be more productive for themselves and the company. How often do we send people to exercise, and then they never implement what was learned? It may have been a mismatch of the right training opportunity.

Quadrant 4: Not Urgent, Not Important
These are your time wasters. If your metrics do not measure what will get you to your goals, they simply waste your time.

As a part of defining what you want to measure, be sure to identify *how* you plan to measure it. On the football field, we start with two-goal lines (the end-zones). From there, we have hash marks every 1-yard. We measure progress during a football game, indicating the overall score, where you are at on the field (compared to the goal line measured in yards), and time left in the game broken down into quarters. Setting up clear measurement points ensures that everyone in the game is using the same metrics and are playing by the same rules. The same should apply when establishing metrics with SWP.

Access Data

With metrics defined, identify how you will collect data in an accurate, reliable, and consistent way. Depending on the metrics you use, obtaining and measuring it may range from easy to complex.

Your goal is to streamline, not create more work for yourself and your team. You don't want to set up such a complicated system that it requires another full-time employee to track, measure, and report your metrics. Tapping into current methods to identify existing data is ideal. Routing those sources of data into a centralized dashboard is even better. The less you must create or recreate, the better.

Reporting

To our adage, "That which gets measured gets done...that which gets measured *and* reported, improves." The point of metrics is to monitor, measure, and improve our outcomes. As data is measured, consider how you will report it and to whom it will be reported.

There are typically multiple levels of reporting for any data. HR must have the raw data to describe the entire story. At the same time, HR must avoid analysis paralysis by stepping back and interpreting the "big data" – extrapolating meaning and applying it to the situation. Our job is not to simply pass data along. Our job is to create well-supported meaning and share it with others to assist with decision-making and problem-solving.

From the information received in HR, we can then tailor the reports to senior leaders using strategic language to avoid getting caught up in the tactical that can often sidetrack the conversations and lose meaning and credibility. HR can formulate reporting to managers and supervisors with crucial information specific to their needs for staffing, development, and production. As each stakeholder receives the correct information in the right way, they will be supported with better data, more timely responses, and the ability to respond to competitive pressures more readily.

Select Solutions

In each of these steps, HR cannot rely on the "old ways" by pulling out an Excel spreadsheet to manage these metrics and reports. Going back to our last discussion on digital transformation, we need a better solution to optimize our performance when it comes to SWP.

The first challenge HR typically chokes on is systems. Systems cost money, and they have a difficult time getting this through financial approvals. I know – I've been there. At the same time, they are the key to making your people far more effective.

Integrated systems can tie everything together. They tap into your business ERP to source data from production, sales, and other operational data. These systems can also tie together all aspects of your HR systems, including staffing, time and attendance, assignments, performance, competency development, learning, and development. When monitoring and managing all aspects, it can become complicated to tie this together without a robust system.

Using an effective system can automate reporting – or at least facilitate it. A best-case reporting option includes real-time dashboards with continuously updated metrics of employee data. Imagine a heads-up display showing staffing, production levels, performance, and efficiency rates. Scheduling can be easier with real-time attendance, time-off management, demand management, and production capacity planning. Recruiting can be largely automated, interviewing enhanced with AI assistance, and onboarding more effectively through competency-based placements.

Choosing the right system can make all the difference in streamlining your administrative burdens (and allow you to focus on the transformation efforts). The wrong system – or no system – can do the opposite and tie you up with admin to the point that you become entirely derailed from any transformation you attempt.

Change Leadership

Credit is due to John Kotter in driving the principles of leading change with his 8-step modelii. Though these principles have been around (and built upon by many) for the past few decades, few have mastered the ability to create and lead it. Instead, we find ourselves managing the change that is thrown at us.

We find this to be true in the world of HR. Change happens, and we are called upon to mitigate and pivot to adapt and navigate our people, practices, and leadership through the rough currents that result. Our role has been primarily reactive when we manage change.

Peter Drucker figured it out years ago when he said:

"One cannot manage change. One can only be ahead of it."iii

That is leading change.

Far too often is HR called in after the plans are made and even implemented. Only after the shifts have taken place in business resulting in changes to people, practices, and leadership is Human Resources notified - typically to mitigate the challenges that resulted from the change effort. This results in managing change from the inside.

Similarly, we stay abreast of changes happening outside of the organization. With changes to employment laws, labor trends, and market shifts, it is critical that we know what is going on and recognize its impact on our workforce. Waiting to be asked for our opinion and how it affects the business is not leadership. Instead, we continue to manage change from the outside.

But in the volatile state of upheaval that we live in (and have lived in for decades), change is just a norm. Maintaining a reactionary approach where we manage the change that is thrown at us means that we are trying to win the game by playing defense all day. To win, you must drive a solid offensive strategy and lead the change on the field. The one who controls the ball most on the area tends to be the one who wins the most during a season.

Building Your Offensive Leadership Strategy

I had just jumped into private consulting – working out of my home at the time – when I got the call. We had signed my 8-year-old son up for tackle football, and we were excited. The call was simple: "We have some good news and some bad news. The good news is that he is on a team. The bad news is we don't have a coach." And then it began.

I played football, knew the sport, loved it, and was a dad. How hard could it be?

This was the start of a 13-season journey with my two sons. As I held my first parents' meeting, it was clear that I was out of my element. While I thought I was well organized, the questions they asked made it clear that I was not. I found my new best friend – Darrin – who was one of my Assistant Coaches for the next 4-years. Once we hit the practice field and saw the size and number of kids, we realized we had a new set of challenges. Not only were we not experienced, but our kids were undersized, and we only had 17 of them (compared to other teams with 24 kids).

Admittedly, the first few games were a disaster. We had some plays set up, practiced hard, and ran the kids through drills, but we had fallen into survival mode. Our strategy had been trying to figure out what was coming next – how big the next team was, what offense they would play, or how to configure our team to match theirs. We were *managing change*. And we lost EVERY time.

It took us a bit to settle into our roles, but the saving grace came as we recognized the part of the proactive mind shift and building a leadership strategy. Once we started to drive the change – to make the most of what _we_ could do and not focus on what the other teams were doing to us – we started to change. The kids grew in confidence, they began to have more fun, and their performance increased.

We recognized that we couldn't show up to a game and "wing it" or defend ourselves to a win. Luckily, we never did, but we also recognized that we had to get better each week. What we did during the week affected how we played the following Saturday. How we coordinated and practiced our plays affected our performance. Training mattered. Exercises mattered. Communications mattered. Even parent coordination mattered.

We weren't perfect, but at the end of the four years, we had won more games than we lost, our kids had fun, and we had formed lifelong friendships.

You can't go into a game in sports thinking that you'll defend your way to a win. In business, the same thing goes – you can't cut your way to profitability, and you can't mitigate your way to goal achievement. It takes a shift to proactive leadership when it comes to addressing change.

Today's business climate breeds change. If you are still talking about change as though it is something outside of the norm, it's time to catch up. Unfortunately, most of our internal structures, mindsets, decision-making patterns, and management strategies are still built around models that are decades old. It's time to evaluate our approach and make the shift.

Creating a Structure for Change

Part of leading change requires us to develop systematic methods to look for and anticipate change. HR leadership transformation requires a shift in mindset from rigid compliance to "what is" to an opportunistic mindset of what "can be." Traditional HR (1.0) focused heavily upon administration and adherence to rules, policies, and regulations. While HR 2.0's business partnership emphasized flexibility, it was not flexible enough to deal with the rapid onslaught of changing parameters faced by today's managers. We need to shift the structural elements that support our transformational leadership to drive business outcomes.

Mindset for Change

As we shared previously, shifts in behavior can change outcomes, but it takes a different mindset to support lasting change. Before we can create lasting change in the organization, we must shift our mindset and our team's. Walking into transformation is not easy. You are going to face an uphill climb no matter who you are. Resistance will emerge from all sides – even if this is the best thing that could happen for you, your departments, and the company.

Let's face it. Everyone likes the status quo. Change is uncomfortable. This requires us to do something other than what we are used to. It requires us to learn a new skill, change our behavior, and achieve something different. The biggest reason for failure in transformation is starting off thinking that we can "wing it" or that it will just happen. It doesn't happen that way. Like any other significant change process, it requires preparation – the most significant one is to decide to create the shift and transform.

Making a Plan

Your ability to make it happen will depend on creating a transformation strategy. Rarely does anything happen through randomness. You must order the steps that will lead you to where you want to go. You may not always know each of the steps that you will eventually take to get there – but you must begin with the framework.

Your first step is to identify what you want – how you want to transform, what problems you plan to tackle, the platform you plan to build, and the resource you intend to be. Consider the resources you currently have and what you need to achieve those outcomes. Layout your game plan over the next 12 months, two years, five years, and beyond. This will serve as your guide for you and your team to take the steps forward through the transformation process.

Create the Right Metrics

Remember what we've said: That which gets measured gets done. That which gets measured and reported improves. This takes us to metrics.

The use of data analytics in HR transformation is essential. Keeping your eye on progress means maintaining a pulse on your progress – evaluating where you are compared to where you are headed. This requires clear metrics, measures, and milestones to determine what you want and what is to be accomplished. Ensuring that you measure the correct data is key to success. Spend sufficient time to evaluate what you want to achieve and determine how you will know (objectively) when you reach your destination. This should help you describe and define the nature of the metrics you will need to measure along the way to make the critical determination in the end.

Set up the key performance indicators that will help you to retain your focus. Assign champions who are charged with aligning various elements of your plan with designated metrics. Set their personal goals to those metrics for accountability, performance, and compensation standards. Develop a reporting system that provides a live dashboard to deliver up-to-date analytical output for you to measure real-time information continuously. A little bit of data obsession is good for the soul when it comes to creating a wholly transformative culture so you can measure the change and demonstrate the value you are adding.

Streamline Policies

Next, ensure that your policies *support* your strategy. The purpose of policies is to create consistency as they support and sustain your company objectives. As one manager shared, "If I have to do something more than three times, I'm going to put a policy or procedure in place to make sure that we do it the same way." Some efficiencies can come from consistency, so we don't reinvent the wheel.

Policies sometimes evolve to become uncompromising standards that are interpreted to apply in all situations. No variance is allowed regardless of the conditions.

In other situations, policies are used as a way to control bad behavior. When somebody does something wrong, they create a policy to make sure that nobody else does it.

In any of these cases, I have never seen a "proactive" policy. They are typically reactive. Unfortunately, they tend to focus on what you can't do rather than guiding you on what you should do to optimize outcomes.

If you're like most, policies and procedures were written years ago. Perhaps your employee handbook is updated annually to reflect changes in employment law, but when was the last time you re-wrote your entire handbook to reflect your culture? Most policies are written following a standard format that is attorney-approved that uses language that real people don't use. Words such as "shall," "may," and "will" are laced throughout the document to insist on compliance.

The problem with this kind of approach is its inability to adapt policies to managers' situations, especially in today's climate. HR preaches the need for strict compliance, but when the policy does not allow for flexibility to meet the needs of the circumstances in a volatile world, it no longer serves as a tool. Consistent application of policy is essential for fairness. Still, when it hinders the ability to use common sense in applying fairness or supporting the good of the business, it's time to change.

HR must evaluate policies to create flexibility to meet the needs of the business. Policies should facilitate business results – not hinder them. If you find that managers cannot accomplish what is needed due to company policy, it's time to change. Creating guidelines that allow for flexible options helps managers govern themselves in different situations and can provide for various circumstances.

If you're not quite ready to give up the complete structure of your current policies, that is understandable. Lawsuits have not decreased, and we still have to protect ourselves. Progressive organizations that train their managers well have lightened up on the details in their policies and have instead provided guidelines with structure. However, if you are still using detailed procedures, consider expanding the training for your managers to give them more options for greater flexibility, faster response, and greater resilience to respond to the changing environment within which they must manage.

To shift to HR 3.0, HR must focus on two areas: (1) to reduce the number of policies and (2) streamline existing policies. Fewer policies provide greater freedom for managers to make decisions appropriate to the circumstance. Teach managers correct *principles*, let them govern themselves, and then hold them accountable for those decisions. For policies that do remain, make them clear and easy to follow. Reduce the jargon, simplify the language, and eliminate the legalese.

Agile Processes

A process is a series of steps to achieve a particular end. When you want to hire someone, how many steps does it take from start to end? Most organizations still have far too many steps that take too much time, involve too many people, and are too complicated.

HR must adopt an agile approach to innovate the way it does business. Just like operations, research, sales, and production are responsible for bringing new ideas to market, HR must find ways to deliver new services and improve the way HR is done. Helping managers and employees get HR "done" better, faster, and cheaper is a primary focus of HR 3.0.

We'll explore more of how continuous process improvement can drive change leadership. For this part of our discussion, recognizing that building agile processes that facilitate responsiveness and adaptiveness of activities and structures to support the organization is critical to lead HR functions that can drive overall performance. Cutting out steps to save time, reduce bureaucracy, and improve the delivery of products and services is a critical component to your competitiveness.

Feedback Response Structure

Another structural component for success in transformation is a responsive feedback system. Feedback is needed from multiple areas to identify how transformational efforts are perceived and their effectiveness.

Establishing clear KPIs and metrics to measure outcomes from transformation efforts can help to evaluate actions.

Provided the transformation efforts are focused on the correct areas and the metrics measure the right data points, these analytics can provide immediate and objective feedback that allows HR to determine how their transformation efforts are working.

Building interpersonal feedback loops are also essential to tap into perspectives and opinions from those who matter most – the people. These feedback loops may come from internal net promoter scores (NPS), employee engagement surveys, micro surveys, post-service surveys, individual responses, and other tools that may be available as effective data collection options. Collecting feedback from business partners such as managers, executives, and other leaders throughout the company is critical to maintaining alignment with meeting their business needs. Using multipoint feedback to assess ongoing performance through the transformation process will help to maintain a leadership position.

Continuous Improvement in HR

We're familiar with the term continuous process improvement. However, we generally limit its use to production, manufacturing, or technology. We're going to apply it to our transformation efforts in HR.

At its core, process improvement is making a process more effective, efficient, or transparentiv. When it comes to HR, ALL WE DO is process!!! Think about it. Forms, meetings, steps, requirements, training, etc. Yes, we add value, but most of the "stuff" we do is through *process* – and as people complete our processes, ideally, they become better for it. They improve their circumstances through promotion, higher pay, improved benefits, better performance, etc.

To improve HR, we must improve the processes that drive it. This will take more than simply deciding to do things differently. While mindset is essential, it is not enough to make that change. We will need a set of tools, methods, and techniques to enhance operations and our environment. In the end, it seeks to refine HR's essential systems to meet the changing needs of employees, managers, and the company.

The goals of process improvement are to:

- Improve employee satisfaction by delivering the right services at the right time, more efficiently, and more effectively than ever before.
- Streamline operations to create new efficiencies that can save time and resources.
- Deliver consistent quality to all employees through improved programs and systems.
- Reduce waste, lower costs, and increase the performance of program delivery.
- Increase communication and connectedness.
- Generate higher employee morale.

To transform the company, HR must first transform itself through continuous improvement. As they provide an example to others, HR stands out as the natural leader in helping the company identify the best path to move forward.

There are nine areas that HR must incorporate as a part of its continuous improvement strategy to lead companies through HR 3.0 that are outlined in the following segments.

Quality

HR's transformation is not only about being different - it's about being better. Process improvement values quality from process creation to retirement. This includes evaluating the process itself, the people involved in the process, and the technology to facilitate it. Continuous improvement should focus on better outcomes for employees, managers, customers, and the business.

Leadership

Process improvement must focus on visionary ideas that can improve the organization and everything therein. Members of HR and those who drive its initiatives must communicate and inspire a clear and compelling vision for the future and how its initiatives can improve the lives and outcomes of those who touch it.

Communication

Communication becomes a part of process improvement as it engages others at a higher level. It involves more people at more levels of the organization than ever before. It recognizes that people in all parts of the organization have opinions, ideas, and experiences that can help HR innovate its designs and deliver its services.

Respect

HR develops greater respect through continuous improvement by building stronger and more collaborative working relationships with others throughout the organization. Continuous improvement allows HR to work with more people, managers, departments, and organizations both inside and outside of the company. By engaging more people, HR comes up with more and better ideas to incorporate.

Discipline

Following a disciplined approach and process improvement activities helps to ensure a thorough and robust solution. Several process improvement efforts fail when a scattered approach is attempted. This is common when those who are new to process improvement want to change everything all at once without following sound methodology or bypassing established best practices.

Enterprise Perspective

The most successful teams implementing transformation recognize the organizational impact of their efforts. They realize that it's not just about them – the HR department. It's about everyone both inside and outside of the organization. What they do affects employees, their families, customers, and others. Ensuring that process improvements meet the needs of those directly involved and the larger enterprise ensures that time and money are not wasted by deploying and then redeploying solutions.

Service Orientation

Effective process improvement values the notion that process improvement activities provide a service. HR must begin the process with the right mindset – with a service orientation to do what is needed for employees, managers, and the organization.

Continuous Learning

Let us be honest – you probably won't get it right the first time. That is why we call it "continuous." Our hope is that along the way, we will get it right somehow. Process improvement values training and education for our HR team to continue to grow. It also respects the ability for us to teach others what we do, how we do it, and to make them better at doing HR. Remember – we don't "do" HR. We only facilitate it. The better we can help others improve their ability to do HR, the more effective we become. When it comes to process improvement, the better we can improve processes to help them do their job better, the more effective we are.

Human-Centered Design

In the end, our focus should be on making life better for our people. Yes – we want to increase efficiencies and overall effectiveness of delivering our HR services. HR 3.0 is focused on making human resources more human. Helping to meet customer requirements faster and more efficiently is what this is all about. Improving performance and motivation across all business areas will help us shift into a leadership position. Continuous process improvement can help us to get there.

Leading the Change

So how do you lead the change?

Let's consider two approaches that can serve as examples and apply them to an HR 3.0 model.

Maxwell's Approach

I've shared that while attending a conference a few years ago, I heard John Maxwell share his definition of leadership. Having been a student of leadership for many years, I have read my fair share of books and definitions on the topic. It seems like there are many ways to define it, describe it, and overcomplicate it. Maxwell seemed to bring it down to its simplest form as he defined leadership as *influence*.

Perhaps the reason this definition made sense was because of my experience as a change agent. Early in my career, I had prepared and rolled out the "from the top" change initiatives. These were well prepared-programs with PowerPoints, flyers, and emails. They included management training and everything else needed to prepare and implement a change program. Unfortunately, these kinds of programs would often fail after only a month or two. They often would not get the traction of those for whom I needed to adopt the program.

Despite my best efforts in planning, organizing, and implementing the program, they just never got traction, and they failed. Sound familiar?

After a few times of doing this, I finally had a mentor who shared with me why these would fail. He repeated the adage that my grandfather would share about leading a horse to water but not being able to make it drink. In other words, you could roll out the program, but you can't force them to do it. He then shared the next part of what I heard my dad say on occasion, but I never really gained the context until this point. He shared, "but you could add salt to their oats." By this, he meant that you could lead a horse to water, and you can't make it drink, but you could indeed find ways to make it thirsty and make it want to drink without them knowing that you're making them want it. That, he said, is influence.

From that point on, I took different approaches to roll out change initiatives.

Remember – in HR, you have access to everyone. In your role, you can talk to anybody, anywhere, at about any time about anything. This is where you start the conversation about change. Following Covey's advice to "seek first to understand, then to be understood," find out what their pain points are and find out how you can provide relief to them. Avoid solving their problem in the first conversation.

However, throughout your conversations, drop recommendations and ideas.

As you get to visit with people, you'll recognize that there are several who have the same problems. If you got them together, chances are good they could solve each other's problems. Soon, you can become the broker to bring people together to start solving issues internally. You may simply facilitate discussions about topics for which you would typically not be a part. During these conversations, you can introduce ideas, make recommendations, provide suggestions, and promote new strategies. These become the foundations for new programs.

Working your networks behind the scenes helps to build this influence on an interpersonal level. As they become your advocates, they will help to promote your agenda and support your programs. They can also help you develop better programs, provide key input, and support your strategies that can drive success.

In an HR 3.0 world, this approach needs to be done faster. The one-on-one approach is still the best way to do it. With an overdose of Zoom meetings, texts, emails, and electronic buzzing, the personal touch rules. Even if they are remote, finding the opportunity to personalize the conversation with a face-to-face engagement will help engage the other person. This greater connection builds relationships that are stronger, deeper, and will help you achieve greater support from others.

If you have done your homework in the previous steps, have a clear plan of action, and communicate your vision, others will jump onboard as promoters and supporters.

Kotter's Approach

One of the most referred to models for leading change is John Kotter'sv. For decades, we have referred to his eight-step process to initiate and execute change management. While I am a fan of the eight steps and have used them over the years, let us consider them in an HR 3.0 context.

1. **Create a sense of urgency**
   In this step, we help others see the need for change through a "bold, aspirational opportunity statement" to show others the importance of acting immediately. Each organization is different. Each situation is different. HR 3.0 calls on you as Human Resources professionals to identify the urgent problems in your organization that you can solve. I find that many times, the greatest challenge to solving the problem is to define it clearly. If I can take the time to explain it well, it becomes easier to solve. Suppose we can clearly define the problem, create a sense of urgency, and demonstrate the need to act quickly. In that case, we can press forward as leaders to guide the organization through the necessary transformation.

2. **Build a guiding coalition**
   Nothing is truer than in HR when we say that you can't do it alone. In any situation, a coalition of influential people – influencers, talent, and other leaders – can

help propel your transformation. Because of HR's perception within the organization in most cases, it's going to need a coalition of internal leaders and representatives from throughout the business. This helps you gain credibility, but it also helps establish the foundational strength to build momentum and establish the foothold you need throughout the organization.

3. **Form a strategic vision**
   For people to buy in, there must be a clear vision of how the future state will be different from the past and its value. You must also clarify how you intend to make that happen. You may not need to have all the details ironed out, but you need to have enough to make it believable, achievable, and motivational.

4. **Enlist a volunteer army**
   For transformation to happen, this will require both heart and mind. Large-scale change requires a shift of the masses. Recruiting a large group of volunteers to promote your cause and actively engage in your movement will create a grassroots campaign to sell loyalty and trust in the new reality.

5. **Enable action by removing barriers**
   As your initiatives begin, your primary efforts must focus on removing barriers to success. Eliminating drags such as inefficient processes and hierarchies can create the flexibility, freedom, and resiliency needed to break the silos and engage collaboration.

6. Generate short-term wins

   The big wins rarely happen all at once. Instead, a series of more minor battles are won and culminates in winning the bigger war. The transformational leader will find opportunities to create success, celebrate achievements with others, and build credibility along the way. This will help to improve systems, structures, and outcomes. These must be recognized, communicated, and tracked to energize the volunteers to continue.

7. Sustain acceleration

   As others see and recognize the success, they will continue to build momentum. This, in turn, will allow for even faster change.

8. Institute change

   As the transformation becomes apparent, it's time to lock in those changes. By communicating how the new behaviors relate to the recent success experienced by the business, HR can strengthen the use of the new practices until they completely replace the old ones.

First Steps

If you read this section and think that you are not the one to lead change, do it anyway. Many of us suffer from imposter syndrome – thinking that we're not ready enough, smart enough, or capable enough to jump in and make it happen. The truth is that none of us are ready to do it when the opportunity arises.

The time is suitable for the transition into HR 3.0. Your organization is counting on you to help them through it. The world is not getting any less volatile, and the need for leaders to step up has never been greater. HR has proven itself a trusted leader and demonstrated its ability through the pandemic to drive the organization through crises. Now it's time to take those same leaders through proactive growth as it seeks to navigate the uncertain waters that lie ahead.

Now is your time. Grab your planning board and begin now.

Management and Strategy Development

HR 3.0 calls for a different approach for managers to manage. HR professionals can drive that change by providing managers and leaders with the tools to make it happen.

Management development has typically fallen under HR. The primary emphases of professional development, preparing new managers, continuing executive development, and other learning and development efforts are common functions. We run our up-and-coming high-potential employees through development programs, orient new managers, and help veteran managers stay current in their competencies.

To transform your business, you'll need to bring your managers and leaders to a new level. They will require new tools and skills to navigate today's challenges successfully. HR has an opportunity to drive this transformation in two critical areas: Management Development and Strategy Development.

Management Development
For HR to transform, it must help the entire organization to transform. Managers are ideally placed in positions of influence to make changes throughout the organization. Leaders must shift from managing to transforming people, practices, and operations at all levels. HR 3.0's vision provides leaders the tools to do it.

Strategy Development
HR must step up to take on a new role in strategy development. This is more than simply participating in the strategic planning process. That part is relatively straightforward (and if it is not, you should go back and work on that first). Strategy development happens at all levels. Each division, department, and manager should know how to develop their strategy that aligns with the organization's primary objectives. HR must serve as the internal expertise to help leaders transform their operations by aligning talent, resources, timelines, and execution plans.

Most businesses do not have the luxury of an on-staff strategy expert. HR is best suited to actively take on this role and assume the transformational leadership position to drive people and leadership to new levels of success. Let's consider how HR 3.0 practices can integrate management and strategy development practices into learning and development to prepare your organization for transformational success.

Transformational Management Development

A critical shift is HR's role and approach in developing leaders and managers. HR has always been linked to leadership, management, and professional development. Whether or not Learning and Development is housed in a separate department, most organizations either accommodate the function within or have a loose connection tied to HR. So how is the topic of learning and development transformational?

When it comes to management development, we've typically connected this to the systematic process of creating effective managers. An organization's approach to developing managers should include a consistent effort to instill knowledge, skills, attitudes, aptitudes, and general competencies to prepare them to execute their role effectively. Ultimately, the goal of such programs is to enable managers from any level to become more effective in getting work done through other people and achieving the organization's goals.

For HR to be transformational, it must initiate transformational leadership throughout the organization. The concept of transformational leadership is not just a transactional model – but a transitional model that permeates what we do and how we do it. Because of the impact of example, transformation must begin with leaders and those in leadership positions – namely the managers and supervisors.

A transformational leadership development program helps a manager:

- Understand and lead with their style. Everyone is different – we all have strengths and weaknesses. Rather than focusing on creating a homogenous approach to leadership, let's fix the flaws holding us back, find out what we're good at, and optimize those strengths for the good of the business and our people.

- Influence others with the most impact possible. Recognizing that leadership is influence, transformational programs will help leaders understand how to optimize their influence to do their best.

- Manage change and complexity in a way that is convincing and effective with others.

- Communicate a clear, positive vision to those they lead.

A solid program will help even the most experienced executive improve. In an increasingly complex, volatile environment, transformational leadership skills can make all the difference in how well a team or business can rise to meet challenges.

Defining the Variables

To help create context, it's essential to recognize the difference between transactional-based management styles and transformational approaches.

In a traditional transactional management approach, the manager is focused on execution – getting things done through other people. While I cannot argue the value in the primary focus of accomplishing the business's goals, the question becomes how to optimize that performance. Under traditional management models, we focus on the five primary areas of planning, organizing, staffing, leading, and controlling. Functionally, this works – we can insert variables into the equation, fill in the gaps, and voila! Work gets done.

If the variables were all constant, this approach might continue to work. However, the one variable that is never constant is the human factor. When we defined performance as a *function* of knowledge, skills, and attitudes all influenced by the environment within which people work, this is the nature of that variability. People become the unpredictable variable in the equation. Still, most managers operate under the assumption that the human element can be controlled, managed, and predicted the same way as any other variable in the production equation.

It doesn't work that way. It never has – it never will.

To optimize business performance, we must find a different way – a better way – to align our people and resources. As we understand the people component and how they work, we can apply the appropriate methods for using their talents to the performance equation. This optimization can never be forced. Instead, it must be influenced.

John Maxwell defines leadership as influence. An effective leader does not depend on title or power to get others to do what they want. They simply have that commanding presence where others say, "I'll follow." You know the type. You see them and say, "I don't know what they're selling, but I'm buying." They resonate with confidence and radiate an energy that you want to be a part of. Their countenance screams, "Come join me...together, we'll get to a better place. Trust me!" And you just want to go.

That shift in leadership is more than a different way of planning and organizing. It's a transformation in the way you do things with your employees. It emotes trust and passion.

Before You Start

As you consider how to develop your transformational leadership development program, HR 3.0 recognizes the need to look beyond simple content considerations. Yes – the content must consider the new dynamics to ensure that you cover the right content to prepare learners for what lies ahead. Other parameters must also be considered as you move forward.

Access to Content

Technology is a significant factor in leadership development. Most businesses have access to learning management systems (LMS), but not all are the same (not even close). HR must ensure that it curates and creates content that aligns with the curriculum to develop learning opportunities to guide development opportunities to develop transformational leaders.

Just offering classes over the internet isn't enough. Ensure that you layout your learning objectives, structure the learner's experience, deliver content, test for learning, and hold them accountable for demonstrating competence. This will ensure they pay attention to what they need to know and that you keep them responsible for the learning required for what lies ahead.

Access to learning also means ensuring that managers have access, whether it be to the instructor-led training either onsite or online (or online to "live" instructor-led training), all online courses through LMS coursework, long-term studies such as at a college, or other opportunities. Where technology challenges may exist (e.g., lack of technology or restricted access to wi-fi), alternative solutions will be needed.

Remote Development Opportunities
The pandemic sent many workers home and created a wave of those who now permanently work from home. Part of HR 3.0's challenge is to maintain continuity in keeping this group of remote workers connected, engaged, and developed. Developing transformational leaders extends to these employees – finding opportunities to engage and establish remote workers in a blended workspace is a challenge. However, it will be critical to maintaining a fair and equitable development opportunity to include remote

workers in the mix of those involved in development programs.

DEI Friendly Solutions
Diversity, equity, and inclusion are elemental to any successful program. Transformational efforts must recognize the need for a shift to ensure that programs are fair and offered equitably throughout the organization. This may require new measures and metrics; however, it will also ensure that the business monitors its practices to provide these opportunities appropriately.

Purpose

Having sat through many conferences, workshops, and training sessions, I have seen my fair share of "the good, the bad, and the ugly." Some so-called trainers are there to hear themselves talk. Others are there to take the old Speak and Spell devices' place as they face the screen and repeat what is stated. On occasion, I come across a dynamic presenter who is dedicated to my learning – ensuring that I become a better person or learn something new due to the experience. Unfortunately, that is a rare occurrence. Generally, it is up to me to dig deep into the content presented to determine what I can benefit from as I sit through another presentation.

Be aware that your employees are thinking the same thing. When it comes to managers, they are extra cautious because they have attended more presentations on average than your other employees. They are reviewing your training "opportunities" with greater scrutiny because of their past experiences with bad training (and their previous experience with anything coming out of HR). We cannot simply roll out the banner of "Under New Management" and pretend that they will simply eat up anything that we offer. We need to provide something new and show them that it will deliver on that promise.

To meet that promise, let's consider the purpose of our development programs. The purpose of our transformational leadership program should be to change behavior.

We will transform the business – how it works, how we perform, and what we accomplish. To achieve transformational results requires a transformation in behavior. To achieve transformational behavior requires a transformational approach to leadership development.

Program Qualities

To deliver a program that results in transformation, you need more than the standard uni-directional lecture-based program delivery model. The following are characteristics to incorporate into your L&D programs to help bring your leaders up to a new level.

Active Engagement
HR must actively engage learners to improve adoption and retention of knowledge and skills to help shift behaviors and ultimately change performance. Transformational outcomes require transformational-level learning delivery approaches.

Immediate Application

Leadership development must apply to learn immediately. Development experiences should be experiential and require an immediate application to the learner's current role. If the learner is currently in a management role, they should direct them to take the principles and apply them in an assignment. Transformational learning must combine theory with practice to provide real-world context and help the learner improve adoption and retention of both knowledge and skills.

Use Personal Life Case Studies

Successful programs use case studies and stories about how principles are applied. Stories are effective methods to teach and train others. Our minds understand stories – we remember stories. When we extrapolate the lessons learned and use them in personal circumstances, we apply them even further. Critical application of principles on our own lives, jobs, and events helps to unlock the unconscious. It allows us to go beyond the conscious and lock in elements of emotions, behaviors, and cognitions to affect personal behavior. As leaders learn to apply principles to their situations, they become well versed in scenario-based principles that stick and can be called upon more readily in future cases.

Competency-Based Leadership

A shift to competency-based learning is effective in a volatile world that demands a flexible, transformative approach to leadership. It allows businesses the flexibility to place leaders where they are needed as they are required. Using competencies, individual managers can acquire bodies of knowledge, skills, and capabilities applicable across multiple interdisciplinary platforms and projects simultaneously. This flexibility creates a new model for businesses to use and creates new development opportunities for individuals to gain the experience they would otherwise not have. The individual manager provides unique opportunities for assignments that would never be afforded in a traditional position-based approach dependent upon the next promotion opportunity.

Leadership and management competencies must focus on three primary areas:

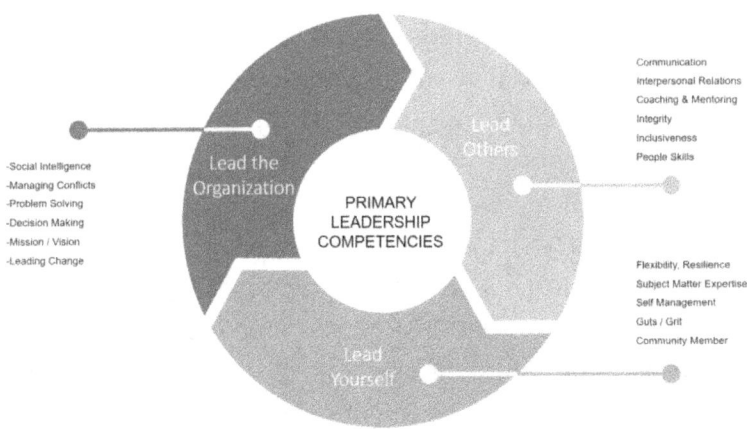

Leading Yourself

A leader cannot expect to lead others if they have not mastered personal leadership. Transformational leadership development should incorporate learning in areas such as:

- *Flexibility*: The ability to manage in a changing, uncertain environment does not come naturally to most. The ability to make decisions without complete information is unnerving. Improving a leader's ability to keep their options open and pivot according to circumstances is critical.

- *Resilience*: The ability to fail is critical. Failure is a part of learning and succeeding. Management and leadership are never about avoiding failure – it's about learning how to fail faster, learn from it, and move forward to achieve goals more quickly.

- *Subject Matter Expertise*: Each manager and leader oversee different departments and functions. While they are not expected to know everything, they should be broadly familiar with their areas of responsibility to give guidance and coaching and recognize requirements for overall department performance.

- *Guts / Grit*: It takes courage to take risks. Today's volatile markets and changing environments create uncertain climates. Risk comes with the job of being a leader. In the end, the leader has to make the call – they need to learn how to muster the courage to make the tough calls.

- *Community Member*: Leaders must become members of several communities. Internally, managers must get involved with other teams, groups of managers, committees, and other gatherings. This is where they learn about what is going on in the organization. This is where they learn the most about what affects the organization. Externally, managers should participate in volunteer positions. They will find that they rub shoulders with other community leaders and will come to network with people in critical positions they would have never met any other way. These relationships will create immeasurable value at some point down the road.

Leading Others

- *Communication*: The ability to communicate both verbally and in writing is key to a leader's success. Those who can communicate effectively get ahead farther and faster than others as they connect more readily.

- *Interpersonal Relations*: Transformational leaders recognize the need to bring everyone along through the transformation. This requires a need to connect with people at heart. Connecting with people by listening, sharing, and building relationships is key to this process.

- *Coaching / Mentoring*: A leader focuses on the development of the other person. This comes as they work to bring out the best in others and help them to develop while working with the team to achieve the business goals.

- *Integrity*: A leader doesn't lie to their people. Period.

- *Inclusiveness*: Just like it sounds – you include everyone. This means treating everyone fairly, looking out for others, helping them when they need it, and providing for their needs when you can. Inclusiveness goes beyond HR's DEI as it becomes an attitude that permeates the culture as everyone feels a part of the team that works together to achieve mutual goals.

- *People Skills*: Collectively, the ability to work with others, engage, meet needs, resolve conflict, and build relationships of trust are all critical factors for success.

Leading the Organization

- *Social Intelligence*: The ability to know and understand oneself and others are important. Self-awareness is perhaps the most essential trait of a leader to respect the norms that govern the culture, interactions, and interrelations among groups and individuals. This will often make or break an individual leader and their ability to interact with others.

- *Managing Conflict*: Conflict is inherent in human nature. It's a part of who we are. An effective leader understands this and handles it appropriately, recognizing the needs of all parties to find a resolution that works most effectively for everyone.

- *Problem Solving*: The best leaders are those who can create collaborative solutions by working with others. The mavericks who think they must come up with all the answers tend to "go it alone" – and are not well supported. Those leaders who involve others tend to gain greater buy-in to the solutions and drive more effective transformation.

- *Decision Making*: Effective leaders can "call the ball." Using the information you have available, understanding what makes information useful, evaluating options, and making a decision is difficult. Few are comfortable with it, but effective leaders can become proficient through practice and experience.

- *Mission / Vision*: Transformational leaders recognize where they are going and have a general idea of how to get there. The vision is clearly communicated in a way that is easily understood by others and delivered in a way that motivates others to want to follow.

- *Leading Change*: Finally, transformational leaders lead from the front.

Other Competencies

The topic of leader competencies has been the subject of considerable research for many years. The context changes based upon the challenges faced, timing, and situations. Ultimately, the leader's job is to ensure the alignment of resources to achieve the organization's goals. While the unique mission, goals, and challenges are different for each organization, common competencies emerge as best practices for the most effective transformational leaders.

The specific competencies vary over time according to market pressures, trends, global pressures, and other variables. Current trends recognize the need to manage a world described by the overly used acronym VUCA (volatile, uncertain, complex, ambiguous). Within this context, The Center for Creative Leadership[vi], Harvard Business Review[vii], and others have suggested the following competencies for transformational leaders:

GENERAL	
General Leadership	• Leadership fundamentals • Theoretical frameworks of management • Diversity, equity, and inclusion • Change management • Cross-cultural approaches to leadership
SELF	
Personal Development	• Understand leadership styles • Develop a personal leadership philosophy • Develop personal leadership qualities • Enhance skills such as decision making, communications, critical thinking, problem-solving • Improve ethical reasoning and cultural competency
Interpersonal Skills	• Enhance interpersonal relationships • Written and verbal communications • Improve active listening • Increase conversational capabilities
Take Initiative	• Practice "courage"
Maintain Exposure	• Improve political and diplomacy skills
Ethical	• Trustworthiness is the most essential characteristic of a leader
Work-Life Balance	• Make life worth living
Self-Awareness	• Increase emotional & social intelligence • Practice reading others' nonverbal cues • Enhance sensitivity to social situations • Exposure to different people and social situations
Career Management	• Manage your career
Self-Discipline	• Maintain control and act out of concern for others. • Recognize possible consequences for your actions.

	- Control natural tendencies to act out. - Be aware of how decisions and actions affect others. - Prioritize needs of others over self - Manage time and energy wisely. - Dedicate sufficient time to self-improvement efforts.
OTHERS	
Interpersonal Development	- Building interdependence in organizational relationships - Develop leadership self-efficacy - Recognize influence on leadership on personal identity (e.g., gender, class, ethnicity, race, religion, etc.)
Leading Others	- Attract, motivate, and develop employees - Serve as a mentor and guide - Focus on teamwork and the ability to be a team player - Set clear goals and objectives with loose guidelines
Confront Problem Employees	- Use direct feedback with employees - Implement radical candor as needed
Participative Management	- Engage employees in conversations
Collaborative Relationships	- Increase influence skills - Work on "soft skills" to engage others non-verbally
Group Communication	- Public speaking and group communication - Improve corporate communication skills - Clearly communicate expectations
Care for Others	- Commit to ongoing development and success - Set a culture to succeed and fail together - Build team into next-generation leaders
ORGANIZATIONS	
Group Development	- Build and manage effective teams - Build relationships of trust - Manage group roles, dynamics, and development - Facilitate group decision making - Share leadership among employees - Develop and maintain organizational competencies - Assist in maintaining overall sustainability
Strategic Perspective	- Understand viewpoints of higher management - Identify strategic initiatives

Fast Learner	• Effectively analyze complex problems • Align people and resources to goal-oriented solutions • Mastery of new technical knowledge • Fast learner and study of business knowledge • Develop extensive business acumen • Industry subject matter expert
Decisiveness	• Learn to make decisions quickly • Identify and utilize accurate data in decision-making • Communicate sources of data to validate decisions
Change Management	• Use effective strategies to facilitate change initiatives • Follow sound strategy to overcome resistance to change • Allow for error – safety for trial and error

Cultural Transformation

Cultural transformation represents a shift that takes place at any level. It may be at the organizational level, but may also happen at the department, team, or individual levels. It goes beyond simply moving desks around, changing out posters, or adjusting the employee handbook. It requires a whole shift in the hearts, minds, and skills of the people involved in the change (e.g., the workforce) to support the culture you want. The change in mindset and shift in beliefs must happen for the required behavior changes to take place for a new culture.

Many cultural transformation initiatives begin and end to motivate, engage, excite, or align employees with company goals. These are significant efforts that are required to support and sustain any long-term shift in culture. Leaders must understand that for culture to transform, it requires a strong foundational shift to support and maintain long-term efforts. As we've discussed, it begins with the mindset to think, believe, and process differently. When your people feel differently, they will act differently – which then results in different outcomes.

The other foundational pillars or supports to lasting cultural transformation include policies, procedures, practices, and norms. If we try to shift mindset without adjusting policies and practices, it's like "pouring new wine into old wineskins." It doesn't work. For the new culture to work, we need a new platform and structure to support it.

Effective cultural transformation efforts.

- **Align** people, practices, and leadership to support organizational objectives and success.

- **Develop** a culture roadmap designed to expedite the implementation of your strategy and the achievement of your goals.

- **Evaluate** the gap between your current state and your desired outcomes.

- **Define** your purpose and values that support the desired changes.

- **Change** policies, processes, and structures that get in the way of your transformation.

- **Create** new mindsets and shifts in behavior through prescribed solutions.

- **Measure** progress toward the achievement of your objectives.

Let's review what it takes to set up our efforts to successfully shift the culture and establish our efforts for the future.

The Foundations of a Culture Transformation

A successful cultural transformation requires full engagement and buy-in from employees, managers, and leaders at all levels. Leaders must model and coach the desired behaviors that will set the new standards. Managers will establish goals and maintain accountabilities according to those standards. Employees will engage their performance and commitment according to the values and beliefs as they align with those of the organization.

Setting a vision for your desired culture is vital and bringing your group of internal stakeholders on board is among your first steps. Once on board, it's time to create your roadmap to lay out an action plan to guide employees through the transformation process. To help you make this roadmap, consider the following questions.

Where are you now?

Identifying your current state identifies your starting point. Transformation is all about moving us from where we are to where we want to be. This requires an honest look at our current state to determine the organization's culture. Relying upon your perception of the culture is not enough. Depending upon an outsider's perspective is not enough. You must obtain a multi-point analysis to get the complete picture of the perceived culture from all stakeholders. Tools such as the following may be used to obtain information on your current culture.

- **Surveys** – Tools such as employee engagement surveys are a great way to collect large amounts of data about company culture. Shorter "pulse surveys" may send out brief surveys focused on only one topic at a time.

- **Focus Groups** – Bring several stakeholders (e.g., groups of employees and managers) to ask them questions about the culture.

- **Interviews with High-Potential Employees** – Visit with influencers throughout the company to get their perspectives on the company's highs, lows, and culture.

- **One-on-One Interviews with Executives** – Gain the perspectives of individual key leaders about what makes the company great or areas that need addressing.

- **Data Analytics** – Review key business data to see how your business is doing today. Review past data to recognize trends and any correlations.

Where should you be?

Identify your desired state. This becomes the goal of your cultural transformation. Knowing what "good" looks like and where you want your culture helps you define your transformational efforts. Setting goals and objectives around your defined destination will help you to know when you have arrived. This may include definitions around market expansion, industry leadership, or customer relations. Describe what your destination looks like: employee engagement, values, standards, and other factors that define the culture as it exists in a "perfect" world.

Why do you want to change?

Define your purpose. The reason for the change should be clearly articulated so all stakeholders recognize why the change is needed and what's in it for them to make the change. If they don't see the value for themselves (personally), they will not be individually committed or motivated to transform. Consider purposes such as:

- Fixing a problem – perceived or real
- Taking advantage of an opportunity
- Expanding into new markets
- Finding, attracting, and retaining new markets

The bigger the pain, the bigger the commitment to alleviate the pain. If you can find the largest area of collective pain for all stakeholders, that becomes the rallying cry for your purpose.

Understanding Where Culture Sits

To transform culture, HR must understand where culture sits in the organization.

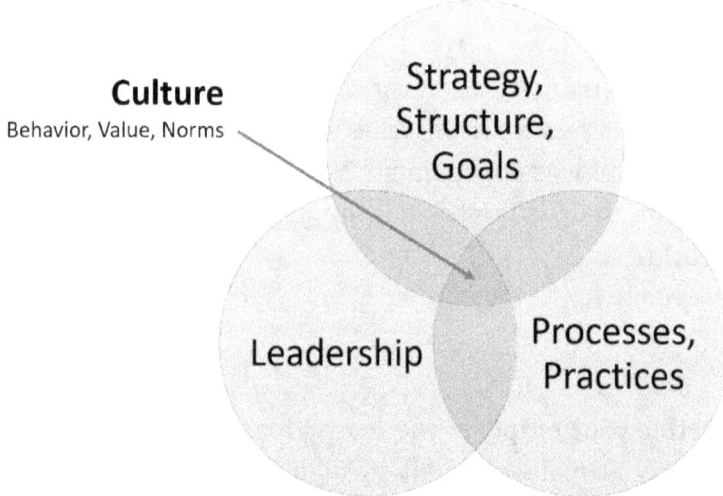

Culture exists where leadership, strategy, and practices merge. Drucker's famous quote, "Culture eats strategy for breakfast" makes sense. Strategy is only one part of the puzzle – it's *what* we do. Culture is *how* we do it. When the practices and leadership are misaligned to what we're trying to work towards, it doesn't matter what our strategy is – the resulting culture will always prevail. It's like trying to drive to a destination using the wrong vehicle. No matter how good your destination (goal) and map (strategy) are – no matter how badly you want it – if the vehicle (culture) cannot get you there because it breaks down or cannot carry everyone to the end destination, it won't work.

We saved Cultural Transformation to be the 6th part of the HR 3.0 model as the culmination of our discussion. We covered the other elements in the previous sections to lay the groundwork for culture. This is where it all comes together. That said, let's spend some time recapping these three overlapping areas that come together to define culture.

Processes and Practices

Processes and practices represent the steps taken to get things done within an organization. These include both the formal and informal such as policies and procedures as well as common practices such as "the way we do things around here." Any formalized approach or adopted steps to accomplish tasks (e.g., the steps to hire a new employee) were created for a reason. Chances are those steps were adopted long ago and are still in place years after they were first established.

Transformational HR evaluates all current practices to streamline processes, revise policies, eliminate steps, reduce or eliminate administration, and increase efficiencies. Processes and practices must align with the company's mission and vision and help facilitate HR's ability to facilitate transformation. If they get in the way, they must be changed or eliminated. It's that simple. HR can help inspire other business areas to do the same and take on a culture of efficiency and agility to better address challenges.

Organizational leadership sets the tone for the culture. Employees cue off leaders' attitudes, actions, words, and behaviors to sense whether change is real or "just another program of the month." Leaders can *sell* the new culture by first adopting the cultural shift themselves. If leader behavior is incongruent with the new culture, a cultural shift will almost certainly fail. The higher the leader is in the ranks, the more influence they have (positive or negative).

HR can influence cultural transformation by working with leaders to buy into a cultural shift. Helping leaders understand the need to change and adopting the new shifts in leadership approaches before launching to the general employee group will help build a coalition to support the change initiative. As the transformation initiative launches, employees will first look to their manager to see their response. If their manager is on board, they'll be more positive about it.

HR can also guide transformational leadership practices. They support the changes in policies, procedures, systems, strategies, and structures through accountability and personal example. HR must demonstrate transformational leadership, starting with their departments. Creating transformational change within HR can illustrate the shift. Creating a new cultural dynamic within HR can lay a foundation for building a broader cultural shift organization-wide.

Strategy

Strategy is simply the plan to achieve the business' goals. HR's role in most organizations is to take full responsibility for aligning employee skills and competencies with the strategic plan. Recall from the discussion on workforce planning that the strategic plan typically gets the bulk of the attention as the entire organization is often involved in its development. The workforce alignment is generally left to HR to manage in conjunction with managers as they connect people, ideas, and resources.

Traditionally, HR serves as the employee advocate to provide direct support to individuals through training opportunities, team building, employee relations, recognition and rewards, growth opportunities, talent management, compensation, and communications. HR also serves as a change agent as they adopt strategic measures and execute strategic initiatives to help deliver required results and outcomes. Strategy is the area where HR can align the efforts of people to work toward the business goals.

In its partnership role, HR provides critical transformation in parts such as succession planning, general employee functions (e.g., hiring, training, orientations, discipline, appraisals), and employee development. Shifting to more data-driven approaches helps them pinpoint where to spend the most time making the most significant impact. HR can guide resources to the right places to achieve goals efficiently and effectively. Recognizing the desired culture can help guide HR in *how* these resources are aligned, developed, and directed.

Culture Shift: What Are We Shifting To?

As with any goal, it is up to you and your leadership team to determine the destination. The funny thing about culture is that if you do not *actively create* the desired culture, you will still create one. Culture exists whether you design it or not. Culture exists at multiple levels.

The leader is responsible for the culture within the span of the group for which they manage and lead. This means that several layers of culture (and several resulting sub-cultures) exist within any organization. You'll recognize the general cultural norms that exist within a company. Then you have the behaviors, habits, and idiosyncrasies within a given department and team. These are all cultures and sub-cultures that develop where practices, leadership, and strategy overlap for each group.

Determining the desired culture is not just left to the CEO and executives. Every leader should answer the same question for the group over which they manage. The principles apply in all cases – they are simply scaled as you increase the scope of application.

HR can lead cultural transformation by helping leaders recognize the type of culture needed to be successful today and in the future. While each organization and circumstance is unique, the following are cultural elements necessary for any organization in any industry to thrive now and in the years ahead.

Agility

When I use the term agility, those who are trained up in process improvement (e.g., Six Sigma, Lean) start getting excited and think I'm going to turn to terms like Scrum teams, Kanban, and work sprints. Agile methodology is an essential step to integrating innovation and adaptiveness in the workplace. Instilling habits of continuous improvement to achieve "better, cheaper, faster" at all levels will ultimately drive customer-centric models that will outperform the competition. However, it does not need to be that complicated, and end-to-end agility cannot exist without the fundamentals in place.

Gallup shared the outcome of a study on workplace agility demonstrating factors that drive agility[viii]. At the heart of agility is a balance between a different mindset and streamlined systems and processes. As we've previously discussed, these two platforms are foundational to the success of any transformational effort. Gallup's factors include:

- Cooperation
- Speed of Decision-Making
- Trial Tolerance
- Empowerment
- Technology Adoption
- Simplicity
- Knowledge Sharing
- Innovation Focus

As HR seeks to instill these factors within both employees and managers, it can lay the foundation for future flexibility, resiliency, and agility.

Learning

Businesses that survive and thrive in today's environment can adapt to changing market conditions, technology changes, and the global sociocultural environment. The companies that adapt win. Winners demonstrate agility to changing market dynamics, and losers see innovation and technology as optional.

With so much change taking place today, organizations must ensure the work culture is in sync with the demands of target markets, consumers, and employees. The ability to create and maintain transformation through such volatility depends on employees and their ability to keep up. They must develop and possess knowledge and skills to keep up and get ahead of the global market changes. This comes from learning.

Creating a culture of learning can help to upskill employees and maintain a continuous trajectory of development. A company's talent pool is critical to determine the overall potential. Continuous learning can prepare people for the rapid transformation required for the dynamic business of today's ecosphere.

Spending inordinate time in classroom training is not the answer. Most organizations already have an integrated LMS (learning management system). These platforms also use technologies like artificial intelligence and machine learning that can predict skill sets needed to grow the organization. Integrating learning as part of the culture can continuously maintain and upskill employees to retain their competitiveness.

Diversity, Equity, Inclusion

The social unrest of 2020 brought about a massive transformation in workplace priorities. There was no escaping the topic in HR. How we responded, though, varied. Some organizations chose to respond proactively with a forward shift toward DEI, promoting inclusiveness throughout the organization. Others hesitated, waiting to see if it was just a fad or if it would stay – and it did. Still, others stayed quiet and held tight to their EEO policies as their introductory statements on the topic, leaning on a compliance-based approach.

Many conversations have been awkward. Many have become heated. Still, others are not happening at all.

I have attended many meetings where we have attempted to discuss the topic. In the groups that appear to "get it," the attendance is typically homogenous with HR leaders from more cutting-edge employers. Most meetings, however, are mixed. I can tell from the body language and silence that we have a long way to go to understand the issue before we can fully address it. For example, some observations I have made are general comments such as:

- Diversity is perceived as a bit "tired" by many, as discussed for years. Aren't we *doing* diversity already?
- Inclusion means not excluding people – isn't that the point of the EEO laws? As long as we're compliant, then we're inclusive, right?
- Equity and equality – what is the difference? If we offer the same things to everyone equally, we can avoid lawsuits – which is our biggest goal, right?

Let's consider the last one – equality vs. equity. Regardless of circumstances, *equality* gives everyone the same resources. *Equity* distributes resources based on the needs of the recipients. Perhaps you've seen a variation of this commonly used depiction:

The example on the left is *equality* – all resources are allocated equally, regardless of need. The example on the right represents *equity* where resources are allocated according to need.

This is a simple visual - too simple to describe equity from an underrepresented population perspective. This example assumes that everyone started on equal footing. The individuals themselves have been blamed for their short height or poor standing relative to the metaphorical fence.

Instead, we now recognize that it's not the person but the circumstances that contribute to their place. Contributing factors such as systemic racism, economic inequality, and other opportunity gaps contribute to an even more significant differentiation of starting points. To achieve equity, the metaphor would look something more like this:

Our ability to transform culture will depend mainly on the ability to influence DEI efforts. This cannot simply be a poster or a speech but must be integrated into company practices, conversations, and programs. What works for your organization depends upon your specific circumstances. However, understanding what you're working toward should help to clarify your approach.

Positivity

With so much focus and emphasis on transformation, let's not forget to have fun and be positive. A Harvard Business Review article shares that when organizations develop positive cultures, they achieve significantly higher levels of organizational effectiveness, including performance, customer satisfaction, productivity, and employee engagementix. Without a conscious effort to instill positivity, a hyper-focused emphasis on performance and perfection can create an overly critical environment where praise is non-existent.

Transformation asks a lot from those who make the change. It calls upon people to move from the status quo to a new state of being. We ask people to leave behind behaviors, habits, and norms to know, be, and do things differently. It can create uncertainty, stress, and anxiety. A sense of hope for improvement can motivate others to do their best and retain their loyalty to the causex. Creating positivity can unite the organization to support the purpose, connect the priorities to personal motivation, and maintain momentum.

Digital Transformation

We spent considerable time discussing the role of digital transformation as an organization and an HR function. A holistic approach to digital transformation is critical to your success – not just thinking about how all the areas come together, but how the organization fits into the overarching ecosystem of industry, society, and all business stakeholders.

The past few years have shifted our goals dramatically. If you haven't done so already, it's time to realign where you want to go, how you plan to operate, what you have to offer, and where technology fits to support all of it. With a real purpose, this approach can build a sustainable growth-oriented future of innovation.

It also means that it's time to be a leader and not a follower when it comes to technology. Purpose-driven technological innovation keeps an eye on the target. Otherwise, when major disruptions emerge, we are easily distracted and go after the next "shiny" object or quick fix to adopt the latest systems and platforms. We may also rush to embrace what the competition is using in the name of staying relevant. Though it is essential to stay abreast of the market, we must let our goals drive the decisions.

The difference between digital leaders and digital followers can impact the bottom line as well. Research from business consultancy, TCS, set these two groups apart by how well prepared and confident they felt in the digital landscape. They found that leaders generated 63% of their revenue from digital offerings vs. 38% for followers.

For those who have yet to shift into digital transformation, it will feel like a significant disruption – a single event to work through. Digital leaders will recognize that it is a continuous status of "digital renovators" as they continuously improve processes to stay ahead of the competition. Digital transformation is never about doing it once and calling it "done." It's all about mindset – setting a vision and going after it to make an impact, share knowledge, or use technology to create a unique offering.

The HR leader must become the digital-savvy leader who embraces ongoing technology advancements and looks for ways to apply them in the organization. The primary goals are automation, user experience, process improvement, and engagement. As you can bring new technology into the workplace that makes employees' lives better and improves business operations, you do your job to contribute value-adding solutions to the business.

As a culture, we have a unique position to influence the adoption of new technology. Bringing in suitable systems to employees can advance processes and help employees to step up their capabilities.

Though I have much more recent examples, perhaps the clearest one comes from years ago at a college. They were preparing for open enrollment. They were still distributing paper forms for employees to complete for benefits selection, and HR was manually processing and entering the final choices for hundreds of employees. I was stunned that we were in the 21st Century and still using a manual process, but I had to ask why. The initial response was that we had employees who did not have access to a computer at work or home, and they did not know how to use a computer. I saw it as an opportunity for multiple advances.

We brought in the online open enrollment system for employees to complete digitally. A series of instructions were prepared via video, e-booklet, and writing to walk them through (and we held a few in-person sessions). We purchased a couple of kiosks to place outside of HR, where we also gave step-by-step instructions. While there was some apprehension that the internet would collapse and the world would end (just kidding), everything went smashingly well.

- HR saved collectively 100's of hours of processing time.
- Employees collectively saved 100's of hours (or more) of time filling out forms.
- We received positive feedback about the new process and its ease of use.
- No complaints. No whining.
- Open enrollment was completed in the shortest time ever and was easiest to manage.

The best win was with Jimmy and Linda. They were a married couple who worked in custodial. They were near retirement and had been with the college for nearly 40 years. They both admitted that they had never touched a computer mouse in their lives before this experience, but this gave them an excuse to do so. They followed our instructions at the kiosks, did it just fine, and they had a good time. It was enjoyable enough that they decided to buy a computer and come into the modern age.

I have observed stories of technology advancement as we have rolled out new HCM/HRIS systems, learning management systems (LMS), and performance management programs. As the process realigns to work well and the system supports it, cultural shifts occur. Processes and systems are structural elements to support culture.

Getting Started: Applying the Change Model to Culture

Remember that change starts with mindset. Transformation comes from a behavior change, but for those behavior changes to last, it will take a shift in perspective to establish the values, beliefs, and thought processes to create a culture that sticks.

Remember – culture comes at the intersection of policy, leadership, and strategy. Where thought, action, and direction align, that defines not just "what we do" but "how we do it."

A complete company-wide mind shift is needed for culture to evolve. Policies can create changes to practices on paper, but leadership must enforce them over time by holding individuals accountable to the new standards. Similarly, goals can be set using the correct terminology, but if staff and leaders are not committed to their achievement, a culture of apathy (or even resistance) can emerge and derail your efforts.

Change in outcomes results from changes in behavior. For the changes in behavior to stick, we need first to change the mindset.

Shifting the Mindset

First, we must shift to the "possible."

Far too often, we pattern ourselves to what is impossible. It's easier to tell ourselves what we cannot do to avoid displeasure. We see any kind of imposed change as a threat and automatically shift into a defensive posture. We approach each new task with distress, causing us either more significant negative stress or a desire to avoid the challenge altogether. Limited mindsets see problems as zero-sum equations where they only have a limited number of resources to work with and a limited number of solutions as potential outcomes.

Shifting to a positive outlook where change is seen as an opportunity or a challenge to be met creates a growth mindset. This perspective offers unlimited opportunities as these individuals call upon the talents of everyone to consider the problem, seek input, and collaboratively facilitate a viable solution. As this approach is adopted organization-wide, businesses instill a willingness to experiment, focus on progress, and create a learning environment that accelerates employee expertise.

Shifting through Influence

In his book *Cultural Transformations*, John Mattone promotes that a cultural transformation at the organizational level begins with the CEO. Most contemporary leadership content will support this doctrine, and I won't argue with it – provided that the CEO will pick up the ball and run with it. This requires the CEO to have a clear and compelling vision, great communication skills, a certain panache to motivate and inspire the masses and align the company's people, practices, and leadership to achieve the mission. *But what if they do not or cannot?*
Enter HR.

HR is uniquely positioned to step up to either (a) help the charismatic CEO accomplish what they need to do to achieve the promises made or (b) step in and drive the strategy to help the business achieve success. In either case, HR brings the tools, resources, and know-how to implement and execute the company's strategy.

Consider this. Just by walking into the organization, you (HR) have more access than anyone else in the entire organization. Remember our discussion about leadership and influence? HR typically has access to company records, files, financials, sales, operations, customer info, and other key data sources. HR has access to information about every person that works for the company – their names, social security numbers, birthdates, kids' and spouses' names, addresses, and more. On any given day as head of HR, I could talk to the CEO, the executive team, managers, the janitor, or all of them together...and it's just another day. No one would think twice about it. Now – who else has that kind of access, influence, and trust? No one. No, not even the CEO.

People don't think twice about us speaking to anyone and everyone. They don't think twice about HR (if we're doing our job right) wandering around, visiting with everyone, discussing strategic, operational, and/or tactical topics...sometimes in the same conversation. It's normal for us in HR to have access to everyone to discuss anything at about any time.

We have direct access to *influence*. What are we doing with this influence?

I don't say this to give everyone license to use this "superpower" for some kind of malicious intent. On the contrary, I point this out to make you aware that you have what you need to step up and make a difference. HR already has access to begin to influence this shift in mindset to align people's attitudes and perspectives towards thinking and seeing differently. We can drop ideas, have conversations, share information, and guide discussions in a way that subtly influences culture shifts. Leadership is influence – step up and be the leader your company needs you to be.

As an executive partner with a strong CEO, HR can step up and proactively guide the subject matter expert on the effective use of talent management and HCM strategies. Helping the CEO understand the impact of human decisions on business results is the ultimate impact on the business's bottom line. HR leaders are uniquely qualified to provide that level of expertise. Through these discussions, HR can guide decision-makers in goal design, competency development to achieve goals, talent acquisition and development to meet competency needs, and metrics to measure and track progress. Such a partnership can help an effective CEO become even more effective, and a thriving company grows stronger.

In a company where the CEO is not as direct in their need to change the company culture, HR can still take appropriate steps to influence the culture to help the company achieve success through active engagement efforts. How HR builds its programs, engages employees, and executes its strategy can have a compelling outcome on the workforce's overall morale, attitudes, and perspectives.

Action Steps

Consider a few examples where we can apply transformational approaches to create cultural shifts. Transformations may be made through:

- **Strategic Planning**: Strategic planning may be standard practice (e.g., annual updates) or a special occurrence that coincides with a new initiative. In either case, it is a time when the company re-evaluates its current mission, vision, and goals for the long-term and then aligns its mid- and short-term strategies and operations with achieving them. This is a time to voice your opinion to shift culture and mindset among critical influencers.

As a contributor to the strategic planning process, be an active participant in the process. Partner with colleagues to provide insights and perspectives regarding talent and its connection to strategy and resources. When appropriate, establish as commanding a presence as the other primary players in the room who represent finance, sales, marketing, and other vital resources. After all – you represent the most core elements of the business.

If you play more of a key role – or if strategic planning does not happen and find yourself in an organizer role – don't shy away from your responsibilities to take a leading role in the process. Step up and represent the people component of your business. Don't be afraid to be bold, but not overbearing, to remain a strong leader without appearing to take over.

I have learned that my involvement in strategic planning becomes what I make it and is dependent upon my preparations. If I have developed my strategies where I have connected HR to the company's overall mission, vision, and goals and can present my drafts during the strategic planning sessions, I play a more significant role. When I show up and have not done my homework, I do not play as big of a part.

During one session, I also learned the value of mentoring others to develop their skills in strategic planning. As the third-party facilitator led the discussion, we began the session identifying organizational goals and priorities. We then broke down the priorities of each department. Recognizing that I may have over-prepared for this group (who appeared to be somewhat under-experienced in the craft of strategic planning), I tried to be cautious about asserting *too much* influence.

The facilitator asked about decision-making processes to evaluate each team member's approach – how we would work together to create the new strategic plan. The first responses were innocuous. I shared my approach, which sounded like a mix of gut-check, data analytics, and herding cats, but I explained it confidently. As we circled the room, three others said they inherently came to me when in tight spots and needed to make the final call. Hmmm...both the facilitator and I recognized the same thing. I had created a dependency. That is also a problem.

Strategic planning allows you an opportunity to *influence* but not control the outcomes. You want to create a culture where everyone has buy-in, feels as though they contributed, and develops the buy-in to drive the motivation to achieve results. Your contribution can influence direction and momentum. Then you can serve as a mentor to others so they can learn how to shift their mindset to a proactive, possibility-oriented approach that allows them to execute strategy within their departments.

- **Leadership Development**: HR is typically responsible for leadership and professional development. What better area to imbed new ways of thinking than within the principles and strategies taught to managers and leaders?

When working for a college, I was faced with a challenging culture. It was slow to change, although the change was needed, and everyone admitted it. The President was in a position where she had too many constituents to work with and could not make immediate changes. The faculty wanted the deeply embedded status quo, the administration wanted to change but were uncertain where to go, and the employees were demanding an immediate shift. There was a sense of pressure coupled with powerlessness.

I had implemented periodic management training sessions that were well received to provide a few tools for managers. After considering the cultural challenge, we brought out an enormous tool: The Management Institute. We offered a development course over half-days, once a week for five weeks. We capped the attendance to create a sense of scarcity and promoted the heck out of it. The spaced learning created time to allow the lessons to sink in and be applied in between sessions for discussion from week to week. We also included homework assignments, team projects, guest lectures from executives, and more. It was a fully immersive course to guide them to a new way of thinking and acting as managers.

It worked. While the initial reaction before the course was tentative, the response after the class was off the charts. We not only had a line out the door to sign up for the next one (which we hadn't scheduled yet), but the first group was asking before the final session, "What's next???" We embedded a new way of thinking and being into the leadership development process to shift the culture from within. As they learned new approaches, were able to apply them throughout the course, discussed the application with colleagues, and changed their behaviors, we saw immediate shifts throughout the organization.

Incorporating principles that align with transformative leadership, adaptive problem solving, and agile methodologies can shift the ways leaders and managers see challenges. Helping managers recognize problems and apply new approaches to setting goals, developing strategies, and executing plans can create a grassroots effort to change behavior and mindsets.

- **HR Team Strategic Leadership**: HR has a risk of becoming a bit "elitist." We become trained, certified, and we know our "stuff." No one can tell us what to do. I'll be honest - I get caught up in it sometimes.

I had a conversation about a week ago. The CFO comes into my office and tells me, "You know what I would love to do, is I'd assign HR 3 metrics..." *Wait! YOU would assign ME? You're not my boss! Who are YOU to assign ME!?!?!? You don't know anything about HR metrics! You fight me all the time. What do you know about HR metrics – I've been trained in this. All you care about is dollars!!*

Do you recognize that same inner battle? Have you had it yourself?

I got so set off by the CFO *telling* me what he would assign me that I lost the point of the message. I had to rewind the conversation and go back to the content. As I did some self-reflecting, I had to recognize some things. First, (warning: I'm stereotyping) finance folks are not the most astute in emotional intelligence. He didn't pause to consider how to craft his message before delivering it to be sure it wouldn't offend me. Second, we talk in HR about aligning to business metrics. Third, the CFO ONLY talks about business metrics, so the chances are good that if HE has come up with an HR connection to business metrics, I should listen. Remember - something isn't a good idea until the other person believes it's a good idea. If I have an opportunity for the CFO to consider (on his own) that HR can drive a part of the business, I should listen.

Luckily, I had listened close enough to hear his three metrics, all of which we were already living by, and I had been reporting on for years. However, because it was HR sending the message, finance thought it was invalid. Now that finance thought it was valid, it was OK. Who knows – maybe we chipped away at the metrics over time, and they caught on? Perhaps he talked to someone outside the organization, and these metrics were validated? It doesn't matter.

What matters is that I HAD TO GET OVER MYSELF. How many of us (and our teams) need to get past the HR Badge of Honor to allow for ourselves to shift? We can't change others until we change ourselves.

- **Employee Engagement**: It's one thing to talk about employee engagement. It's another to do it. I believe that the better we can connect to employees, and the more personally we can connect with them, the better we can fully engage them. For me, nothing gets more personal than health, and it can create an excellent opportunity to shift mindset and affect motivation.

When faced with a multi-year trend of double-digit increases, one company was at its wit's end. They presumed it was simply common practice to (a) increase their healthcare budget by as much as 20%

each year, (b) find ways to decrease benefits, and (c) pass costs to employees. This is a standard practice among all employers who manage healthcare.

It was not my first rodeo on this kind of scenario, and they gave me latitude on the program. The first step was to engage employees as partners. They had to know that we were in this together. If we were to control costs, they needed to understand how costs were calculated, so I educated them as fast as possible. Once they learned that claims were the #1 driver of health insurance costs and that health insurance worked like car insurance (e.g., you wreck your car, your car insurance goes up; you wreck your body, it costs money, your insurance goes up), behavior changed. As they recognized that their behavior affected their costs, it was the first step.

The second step was proactivity. We challenged them to be proactive about improving their health. As they did so, we would give them two ways to gain financial rewards: Offering substantial money to offset their deductibles for high deductible plan members (Yes! The entire deductible for them and their spouse!!) and dramatically lower premiums.

Wellness became the banner of hope for personal health and cost containment – for individuals! Instead of pay increases to cover the increases in health insurance costs, employees benefited from a 5-year negative trend (at the time of this book). That means that health insurance costs DECREASED 5 years in a row. We cut employee premiums to be FREE for individuals and families, and it dropped by over 65% over five years. As the company saved money, employees saved money. As the world was experiencing massive healthcare mayhem, this company offered FREE healthcare – free premiums and the ability to earn the ENTIRE deductible through HSA incentives.

As we offered programs to learn more, engage more, and do more, people paid attention. Wellness was at the core of the culture. We talked about it. We paid for it. We built it in. Why? It helped employees and their families stay healthy. It saved employees money (and let them keep more of their paychecks). It saved the company millions.

Give employees a reason to get excited, and they will engage. It's that simple. Just give them a compelling reason to follow you and then drive them toward a compelling vision.

Don't Use the Word "Culture" So Much

Finally, avoid using the term "culture" as much as possible. Even though our goal is to change the culture, it's like any other type of change. People don't mind change so long as they think the idea was theirs. Whenever people hear that *you* are changing the culture, they don't want to have anything changed. If you can put exciting new opportunities in front of them, put things in motion (behind the scenes), introduce new models and solutions, and get their involvement, they'll buy-in. Culture will come for the ride.

Adjusting practices, strategies, and leadership will result in a culture shift. If you can direct those three areas where you want the culture to be, it can get there.

HR Professional: Personal Transformation

The 6-Steps are critical elements to make the shift happen for any organization. Our ability to successfully navigate HR 3.0 depends on the ability of the HR leadership team to adopt and lead these strategies.

At the center of all of it is you – the HR professional.

HR leaders cannot lead transformation unless they first transform themselves.

We call on the HR pro to know more, do more, and be more than ever before. To be effective, the HR pro must lead, adapt, and demonstrate agility at a speed and level like never before. The breakneck speed of change will only accelerate. The pace of competition, new regulations, shifting tide of social reform, workforce demands, labor supply and demand, and technology innovations are just a few of the adaptations that businesses must make.

To lead our teams and businesses through these tumultuous times ahead, we must emulate the change we drive. We need to develop the competencies critical to create and maintain a successful transformation to propel our organizations into the future. Let's explore the competencies required to get us there.

Personal Transformation Drivers

HR professionals can distinguish themselves as transformational leaders by adopting several best practices.

Develop and Deploy New Skills

In our discussion on workforce planning, we talked about the need for developing more extraordinary skills in managing the market, business, and talent. As a recap:

- Market
  HR leaders must stay abreast of what is going on in the marketplace. Locally, leaders must recognize the competition for the business AND labor. Remember that your labor competition may be across industries (e.g., a highly qualified administrative support professional can apply anywhere). State and national trends affect local trends with regulations, labor availability, and impact on commerce. Global demands affect all businesses regardless of type and size. The global pandemic is the most obvious example of how

economic and social connections have an immediate impact on our people and business.

- Business
To achieve transformation, HR leaders must take a deep dive into the business. It takes more than just the SHRM foundational competencies to get by. While they are essential, HR must grow in depth and breadth of understanding financials, operations, logistics, products, services, sales, and other critical business functions. This helps HR to develop greater agility in its solutions to company leaders. How can HR know what talent and skills they need to source for other managers if they do not fully understand what the business does? We need to go deeper in our understanding of the business.

- Talent
Talent management must shift to people sourcing as we consider the whole person and lifestyle, not just the competencies that they bring. While alignment of individual competencies to business needs is still critical, we must also focus on the complete experience (EX) to engage and empower employees to achieve their best. As we bring people into the organization, we can understand their competencies and how they fit within the various capacities throughout the organization. As we understand the competencies needed throughout the company and the competencies held by employees, HR will shift into a strategic sourcing agent of talent to match the right people with the right need at the right time for the right project.

While some may argue that these are the current responsibilities of HR – and they are to a degree – the shift to a transformational approach requires us to become more adaptive and flexible in our process. We must become more resilient and faster in our ability to understand, predict, and respond to markets. HR must use these predictions to forecast labor and provide solutions throughout the business *before* they are asked. From there, HR can source the talent needed in advance of the needs. This is how HR transforms the business by becoming the preeminent problem solver.

Create and Lead a Diverse, Global Workforce

HR leaders are best suited to assemble and direct employees from varied backgrounds when hiring for projects, competencies, and long-term needs within the organization. This creates a balance to meet employee needs, diversity opportunities, and inclusiveness to optimize the work environment.

Transformational leaders recognize the need to be in front of this, aligning internal resources and culture to support equitable workplace initiatives that support forward-thinking transformation. While the theme of diversity, equity, and inclusion are at the forefront of conversation, transformational leaders have already integrated these into the operational functions of business strategies. Recognizing the value that comes from an integrated approach to diversity and the long-term benefits of an inclusive workplace, leaders can offer a workplace conducive to building and maintaining a positive work environment that is inviting to employees. This develops and sustains a high-performance culture supportive of ongoing development and progress to align and achieve individual and organizational goals.

Key Characteristics for HR Professionals

To accomplish what we've laid out, the HR professional will need different tools to move from a traditional and strategic to a transformational approach.

To quote Grandpa, "What got you here won't get you there." If we keep doing what we've always been doing, we'll keep getting what we've always had. If we want to shift into a transformational approach, we need a new system.

The transformational leader will need an improved set of competencies to take HR to the next level to meet the changing needs of today's organization. These competencies must increase in depth and breadth to set the vision and direction of the HR team to make the shift and have the organization follow along.

As the goal of transformation, HR professionals must recognize the desired end state to which they seek to change. If the HR pro can know what "good" looks like and have an idea of what they should be working towards as a transformational leader, that can help create a base to work toward.

Consider the list of leadership competencies outlined in the previous chapter. Those are foundational competencies that are relevant to every leader. In addition, the HR leader must take charge of HR's transformation. You will be required to take on a heavy burden that can be challenging. Every shift away from the status quo (fighting the cultural homeostasis) will naturally bring resistance. Though that resistance is targeted at the fear of change or resistance to leaving the comfortable, you will be the target of that resistance because you're carrying the message.

Being the leader is challenging, especially through any change process.

You must remember why you're doing this. You undertake transformational change for a reason – you want something better. You know there is a better version of this world out there, and the transformation process is the way to get you there.

You are the only thing between where you are now and your desired state. Your first step is to recognize *your* desired end state as a leader. What must you become to lead your team, department, and organization through this transformation? This starts by understanding what it takes to master the transformation. This does not mean that you must perfect these before you begin the transformation process. It only represents the direction you are headed to continue to develop yourself as you lead others through the process.

Consider the following characteristics of an effective transformational HR leader. These qualities can help you establish the foundation upon which you can build these needed competencies to lead the transformation.

Authentic

The HR leader must emphasize building their legitimacy through honest relationships with others. It is leadership that is built upon an ethical foundation with truthful self-concepts, promoting openness and transparency. This runs contrary to those who tend to hide their emotions, agendas, and motives. Instead, the transparency requires the transformative leader to be true to themselves in their role. It requires them to maintain strict coherence between what they feel, what they say, and what they do. Making value-based choices is also a sign of authentic leadership as we do our best to make the right calls by doing the right thing.

Inspirational

Inspirational leadership is the ability to positively influence those around us while motivating them to achieve success. As a transformational leader, we are working towards helping others set and achieve new goals. To help drive their efforts, inspirational leaders tend to be passionate, knowledgeable, personable, and resilient. They engage and respect others by maintaining self-awareness, continuously seeking to set, share, and achieve a shared vision.

Visible

An effective leader leads from the front. They set goals and ask others to follow them – not simply going after a dream they set. The leader is out there *doing*, not just talking. It requires action and visibility to engage with others. Regular communication, participation, and activity are a must for any leader to provide an example to others to achieve the desired outcomes.

Inclusive

Transformational leaders seek to include every person at every layer in the organization. Strength comes in numbers, and the more people involved in the process, the more buy-in and commitment that comes. The effective leader understands that inclusiveness is not just a trend or a mandate but also a competitive advantage that comes as people align their efforts to achieve more.

Be Purposeful

Aligning people and resources to achieve a common goal is the pinnacle of leadership. Continuously working towards a good cause – a common purpose – is the highest calling for a leader. As the leader demonstrates the commitment and loyalty to work towards that purpose, it will inspire others and drive their performance to achieve new heights.

Flexibility

Things happen. Nothing will go your way 100% of the time. Plans change. Disaster may even come. The effective leader recognizes that failure may occur as an ordinary course of the experience. It's not whether you win or lose – it's whether you get up and get back into the game. We must be ready to pivot quickly and adapt to changing dynamics. Building Plan A and Plan B are essential, but plans C through F are handy to have on hand as well.

Agility

We've discussed the need for agility in leadership. It's worth mentioning again. Identifying opportunities for continuous improvement helps to save time, effort, costs, and steps. The agile leader always looks for ways to make it better to improve the experience for them, the team, the business, and others.

Where to Start

As we come to an end, you may ask: Where do I begin?

You may have jotted down several ideas of where to start. I hope you did.

Let me walk you through two approaches to consider as you prepare your new "To Do" list.

Start – Stop – Continue

We use a simplified method using a start/stop/continue process in some process improvement corners. When we evaluate a program, an event, or process, we consider three questions:

- What do we need to START doing that we did not do or forgot to do?

- What do we need to STOP doing?

- What do we need to CONTINUE because it works?

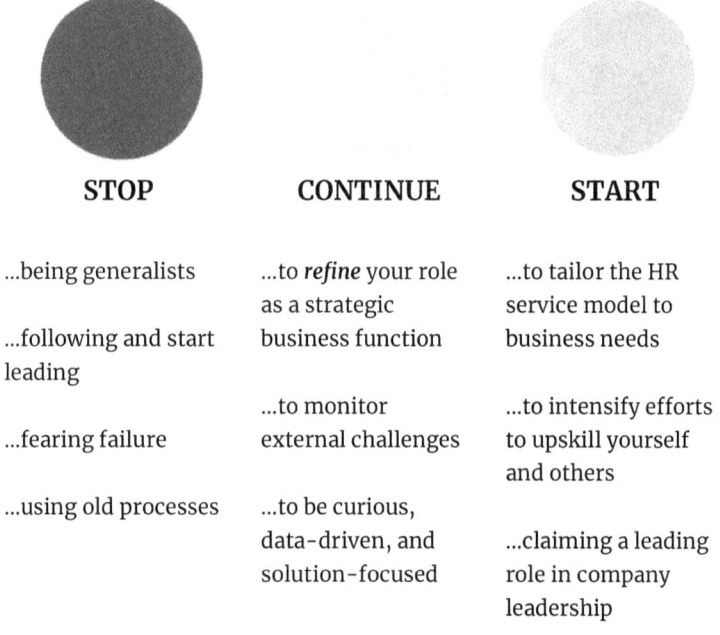

STOP	CONTINUE	START
...being generalists	...to *refine* your role as a strategic business function	...to tailor the HR service model to business needs
...following and start leading		
	...to monitor external challenges	...to intensify efforts to upskill yourself and others
...fearing failure		
...using old processes	...to be curious, data-driven, and solution-focused	...claiming a leading role in company leadership

Your list will be unique to your circumstances. Each business is different, with specific challenges and opportunities. Remember your primary focus areas as you conduct this evaluation.

- **Yourself**

You cannot help others until you help yourself. Stop spending all of your time focusing on everyone else and begin to shift your mindset. Continue to move forward in your partnership with key leaders and start to take more proactive measures to become the leader you know you can be. Stop falling prey to imposter syndrome – believing that you don't belong in the same group as the other executives. You are responsible for the success of the most significant resource the company depends upon for its success.

- **People**
Your strategies, processes, and systems must converge to enhance the outcomes of your people. As they succeed, your business grows. The achievement of your business strategy depends on the success of your people. Stop focusing on the barriers (e.g., policies, processes, and systems that get in the way). Start identifying opportunities to streamline processes to facilitate high performance and help your people achieve their best.

- **Business**
If we want to become business consultants, we must understand our business – what we do, what we make, what we sell, and how we do it. To source the best talent, we need to know what we are looking for. HR professionals must move out of the office and onto the floor to understand what the company does, how they do it, and what is required to be better prepared to find the talent needed for business success.

- **Market**
The global markets are continuously shifting and affect every business, large and small. When HR understands the market, it can prepare, forecast, and manage the supply and demand of available talent. Waiting until the skill is needed before searching for it is a recipe for disaster. Those HR pros who understand the market the best will win at the talent wars.

Your "Top 10" List

Most people enjoy a Top 10 list to generate ideas. Recognizing today's shifts and our move to HR 3.0, what are the best practices that employers are making to transition quickly to become more transformational in their efforts?

Consider these first steps as you develop your HR strategy to move forward in your new transformational role.

Pre-Step: Assessment

Before developing your strategy, take time to evaluate your starting point. Understanding your current strengths, weaknesses, resources, and limitations is essential, so you know what you have to work with. Setting aggressive goals is excellent, but trying to build a skyscraper with only a hammer and screwdriver just isn't going to happen.

Recognizing your initial limitations does not define your destination. It only helps you realize the size of the gap you must overcome to get from where you are to where you want to go. It will not define you; however, it will help you set the parameters by which you can establish realistic milestones and objectives to help you achieve fundamental transformation.

Take time to conduct an internal audit of your current practices and procedures. Evaluate yourself and your staff for knowledge, skills, abilities, and competencies. Recognize what you know today to understand what you will need to learn to achieve your goals. This will help you divide and conquer the learning gap that will be a part of the process.

Pre-Step: Desired State

With the starting point defined, consider the desired end-state. Just saying that you want to be "transformational" or "better" is not enough. Take time to create specifics. What will transformational HR look like? How will it be better? What will you do differently as a result? How will the business be better because of it? How will managers' lives be better? How will employees benefit from "transformational HR" vs. what is offered today?

If you cannot clearly define the outcomes, it will be a tough sell to others. You will not be able to entirely "sell" the transformation to your team, business leaders, or employees. You may not even be able to sell it to yourself. Transformation is challenging – and without a clearly defined vision of how it will be better, you may lose the energy needed to maintain the necessary push to get through the resistance that will come.

However, with that vision, you can create passion and momentum that drives you and your team forward. That momentum will catch fire with leaders, employees, and others who recognize the bold moves and benefits of the differences. Soon, no one will remember that there was ever another way to have done HR.

Your Emphasis

With your vision squared away, it's time to set your priorities. You can decide what to focus on first. Trying to work on everything at once is not adequate – you simply do not have the time, energy, and resources to make it happen. Prioritizing where you can make the most significant impact first will make the most sense. From there, you can identify the next and so on until you work your way through all your priorities over time.

As a transformational leader, it is crucial to focus on what matters most. Based on the collective feedback from several studies, the following list was assembled that covers ten of the most common areas that transformational HR initiatives focus on.

1. **Measure Performance**

Going back to our statement:

- That which gets measured gets done.
- That which gets measured and reported improves.
- That which gets measured, reported, and rewarded, continues.

The first step to this process is to create consistent and accurate measures of what matters most. Data exists from many sources. With the big push in "lean," we tend to incorporate data analytics wherever we can with the thought that if we can apply data – any data – we must be doing something right.

The greatest challenge is not measuring and improving the most overlooked measure that matters most – human performance. We have struggled with this one due to its simplicity and its complexity. The simplicity comes as it requires only that we open our mouths and deliver free, dynamic, and responsive feedback that can immediately change performance, behavior, and outcomes. The complexity comes from the human factor – we are afraid of the repercussions of the feedback. It *might* hurt their feelings, make them upset, affect our friendship, or otherwise make our working relationship awkward.

While those human dynamics may be actual – feedback may result in awkwardness – certain truths exist. First and foremost, *we can't fix what we don't know*. If we want people to improve performance, they need to find out how to improve their performance. They are not going to figure out on their own what needs to be improved. The faster we can help them understand things, improve things, and become better, the better they will become. We are doing them (and us) a favor with the feedback.

Our fear is often being perceived as a jerk by delivering feedback. It doesn't have to be that way. When using a candid, objective approach, we can provide it without the emotional side getting in the way. Following the SBI model created by the Center for Creative Leadership years ago, we can share feedback explaining the situation, their behavior, and its impact. (For more, refer to the SBI model.) Ongoing, continuous, and candid feedback is the only way for people to improve performance fast enough for transformation to happen.

Another concern with performance is measuring the correct standard. When we deliver feedback, there is sometimes a concern about whether we are giving the right feedback – am I giving them accurate information? This comes down to measuring performance using consistent standards. As we establish common goals, identify consistent standards, set clear expectations, and hold others accountable to those standards, we can allow individuals to manage their performance.

Part of transformational leadership is to help others to develop themselves. We must shift away from "managing performance." That takes a lot of time and effort on our part – why manage others' performance? Let them manage their performance. Teach them correct principles, give them the best tools, create the right vision, and then let them perform and govern themselves. Our role as transformational leaders then becomes to coach, guide, and adjust according to the measures and metrics towards which we are moving.

As transformational HR professionals, we must work with our managers and leaders to shift their mindsets. While we have preached these concepts previously, it creates greater emphasis to align systems and practices that help managers to:

- *Coach and adjust individual goals and metrics to continue to align with business goals.*
- *Create shorter goals that lead to bigger goals.*
- *Give continuous feedback.*
- *Implement technology such as mobile apps to allow for continuous feedback through metrics and performance measures.*
- *Hold themselves and others accountable for ratings and conversations.*

2. **Leadership Investment**

Your business is only as good as the people that work for it. We depend upon our people's knowledge, skills, abilities, and competencies to deliver the products and services of our business. Without people, there is no business.

The job of a leader is to help facilitate the success of the people in the organization. It makes sense for us to invest in our leaders to optimize the investment in our people. Investing in leadership creates leverage – a multiplier effect to enhance the outcomes that support the performance and success of all employees. The better we can develop our leaders, the better we can help our employees to achieve their success.

Leadership investment goes beyond simple classroom training or courses they can read in a book. While these may be beneficial as supplementary resources, within themselves, these cannot constitute your entire leadership development investment. Others may believe that leadership happens on its own – with time, leadership skills will develop. All these examples may provide some benefit to leaders; they are not optimal as investments. Your organization can achieve a much faster and more effective ROI by adopting a different mindset and approach to leadership investment.

Investing in leadership should involve an immersive experience that goes beyond the classroom. While it should include the classroom to incorporate theory and practical learning, there should always be an immersive experience to apply real-life situations and scenarios. Ideally, as a leader is in the field, they can apply what they learn at the moment. In a best-case scenario, they may even have a mentor to evaluate and coach along the way. This provides real-time feedback to guide and enable their application of course development content. The hands-on experiential learning approach can allow you to develop leaders using accurate models and to help them through real struggles to succeed, fail, and apply learning to achieve leadership success faster.

Transformational leadership investment opportunities should also consider programs that incorporate:

- *Leadership programs based on performance outcomes (with moving to non-leadership if the continued failure persists).*
- *The role of the leader as a coach and the related skills to apply to employees.*
- *Servant leadership principles.*
- *Behavioral and predictive leadership styles.*

- *Employee engagement scores to develop managers and rank their effectiveness.*

3. Agile Thinking / Design Thinking

Today's world calls for every leader to have the mindset of continuous improvement. Transformational HR strategies are no different. One of the most critical qualities of transformational HR will be the HR team's ability to adopt an agile mentality. Applying design thinking represents strategic and practical processes to design products, techniques, and innovative approaches to rethink HR. It's not just about incremental improvement – it's about rethinking the entire model.

A critical step in shifting mindsets, developing strategy, and implementing change in the organization is to adopt an outcomes-based approach to HR management. No longer will we talk in generalities or be judged by "soft skills" that are often associated with the function. The transformation must shift to identifying specific, measurable outcomes that result from these efforts.

Shifting away from large-scale programmatic changes to more minor releases can help HR make transformation happen at a lower level. Creating these small collective wins at lower levels will culminate into the more significant shift that can gain momentum. This is how HR transforms the engagement process by creating active involvement by individuals, teams, departments, and other groups.

The agile mindset starts by asking how to improve things at the local level. Recognizing that anything and everything can be improved, this mindset can be adopted by everyone in the organization. Implementing a global, top-down approach rarely works the first time. However, implementing this kind of grassroots design thinking method to adopt agile thinking at the individual level can shift an entire culture in a short period.

Taking this approach sounds easy. However, it must be designed, strategized, and built into the processes that you are currently undertaking. It will not happen on its own. Recognizing how to do it and the best approach to achieve it are crucial to your overall success.

4. Pay for Performance

Throughout the years, the concept of pay-for-performance has been strategized, developed, and implemented in many iterations. It has been seen as the cure-all by management to implement change and achieve business goals. Employees have also seen it as the antithesis to all things good and human. If done well, a pay-for-performance system can give everybody what they want – it can reward individuals well for their excellent performance and provide them with what they want and need. If done poorly, it can manipulate, cheat, and take advantage of employees.

At the heart of pay-for-performance is the question of value – what is perceived as valuable to one person is not valued the same as to another. Having a one-size-fits-all approach to rewards is what makes the system fail. Another challenge is the size of the rewards – creating a system with so much promise only to find out in the end that it either offers very little or it does not hold a promise at all and makes employees feel cheated when they arrive. Employees must feel that the reward that they work towards has value, meaning and meets their needs.

In an HR 3.0 world, we recognize that the employee experience is critical. We need to get smarter with employee rewards to provide motivational rewards that add value to the individuals – as THEY view them to be rewarding. Approaching pay-for-performance with a one-size-fits-all approach no longer works. We need to add some variability to the reward mechanisms.

The other consideration is fairness. If people feel that they understand the "rules of the game" and believe that they are judged fairly according to those rules, they will buy into the process. When they feel that they have no control over the variables for which they are judged, they believe the criteria are fixed, and sense that the measures are unfair or that the criteria for judgment are inconsistent, there is no motivation to perform. It typically runs counter to performance and becomes a demotivator.

For pay-for-performance to work in a transformational setting, you may consider revising and relaunching a program with the following criteria:

- Offer variable rewards. Rather than a single structure based on base pay merit incentives, consider a variable

option according to the needs and wants of the employee (e.g., base pay, lump-sum bonus awards, paid time off – one time or accrued, paid vacation).
- Fair and equitable according to objective standards and criteria. While most companies identify the requirements, HR should ensure that all performance and rewards standards are clearly outlined and available to all employees.
- Transparent matrices are available to demonstrate to employees what is available according to performance outcomes. Many employers are afraid to share what is known as it may put management discretion at risk. Consider listing the array of options available and the criteria for performance to set clear standards and expectations of high performance.
- Consider identifying market value for performance according to skill level. Traditional compensation studies evaluate positions based on market value alone. Consider researching the importance of jobs according to performance levels.
- Pay transparency has become a hot topic. While many private sector employers remain tentative about sharing specific information about their pay practices, greater transparency could shine a light on what it takes to achieve the highest levels of compensation based upon individual performance. Provided that managers hold employees accountable consistently, this should help establish clear standards.
- Consider integrating AI to remove bias. Suppose there are performance factors built-in to individual KPIs. In that case, you may be able to utilize artificial intelligence to evaluate individual performance within

those factors and establish a portion or all pay determination according to that assessment. This can help to remove personal bias in pay-for-performance calculations.

5. Professional Development

Professional development is not a new topic. However, to achieve a level of transformation, we need to approach it differently. We need to become collectively smarter than how we face the competition and how we work. Transformational HR is about how to help individuals achieve higher performance through enhanced professional development to meet those needs of the new world in which we work.

We've discussed the need to upscale talent. As a business, we need to learn how to be better, cheaper, and faster. Because our company is only as good as the people that work for it, we need our people to learn how to work better, cheaper, and faster. The better our people become, the better our business becomes.

HR's role is to enhance individual competencies that meet the increased need for business and project competencies. This shifts HR into a different function of developing and sourcing talent in new ways. We are no longer matching people to jobs but rather competencies to specific talents needs. This means that we must break down specific competencies held by people to understand the knowledge, skills, capabilities, and background. We must also be aligned with the business and its managers to understand specific competency needs to recognize what they need, when they are needed, for how long, and at what capacity.

By understanding our role as competency brokers, we can evaluate, measure, and assess the competencies that exist in our organization. We can also stay abreast of the marketplace to recognize what competencies are available and determine future needs. As we effectively forecast demand, we can evaluate requirements to develop specific competencies internally.

For example, recognizing a wave of retirements over the next five years, an HR manager might determine that the business will need to replace several welders in the next two years. However, looking at the forecasted demand, specialized jobs are coming in over the next year. These jobs will vary across departments, and the same demands will cross groups. The work will ebb and flow across groups and require greater flexibility and the need to share resources from one group to the next. Traditionally, HR would hire a specific welder for a single position. Now, an individual must be employed with a given set of competencies to be assigned in different capacities throughout the organization as needed and may require ongoing training to upskill in new technologies to prepare for incoming work to be performed.

Similar sourcing will be required for non-technical positions as well. Management and leadership positions will require flexibility and resilience to move from position to position. These competencies are going to change, and employees must have access to ongoing development opportunities. The HR 3.0 model for development must provide:

- Personalized learning opportunities according to individual needs. Learning is tailored to specific individuals, their competencies, learning styles, and interests.
- Technology can leverage AI and analytics to track, predict, and forecast the supply and demand of competencies among employees.
- Opportunities for employees to choose their track for professional development opportunities and guide their learning experience.
- Immersive learning adventures that go beyond simple courses available through the LMS. A multifaceted approach to development must be offered using online, in person, and on-the-job experiences.
- New learning opportunities incorporating VR, augmented reality, peer-to-peer, internal mobility, digital badging, and other best practices to encourage and reward ongoing learning.

6. Design Intentional Experiences

HR 3.0 enables the alignment of people, technology, and performance. Employees demand more from their work than simply earning a paycheck. We recognize that people spend more waking hours per week at work than anywhere else. The need for work-life balance is critical to maintaining physical, mental, and emotional wellbeing, all of which contribute to employees' ability to contribute to the business' goals. If we want to keep people performing, we need to keep them engaged in the overall work experience.

The traditional tit-for-tat exchange of work-for-pay is one-sided. Employees come to work, sacrifice for the company, and get paid. Transformational efforts seek a better relationship where employees are part of the ecosphere where we work together to achieve success. This requires a focus on mutual success – as employees succeed, the business succeeds (and vice versa). This human-centered design calls upon HR to create engaging experiences that energize, motivate, and fully engage employees.

Transformational HR practices must develop a 2-way dialogue with employees to find out what they want – how we can engage them to be part of the solution to help them achieve success. We must find a way to create safe spaces for them to share ideas, build relationships, and enable knowledge sharing. As concepts are created and collected, these can be used as the foundation to design experiences to enhance the overall outcomes for employees.

As HR works with employees to develop methods to better engage employees through these experiences, implementing a common platform can help to centralize communications, ideas, and efforts. Offering new experiences in benefits, wellness, activities, communications, networking, engagement, and other solutions can shift from simple "employment" to a complete experience. Designing a set of measurable outcomes can help you to identify whether the solution is working through satisfaction assessments, pulse surveys, and other measurements. In the end, the goal is to avoid leaving experiences to chance and, instead, design the kinds of experiences that can influence positive outcomes for employees.

7. Improve HR Tech

If it hasn't been emphasized enough in this book, let me do it one last time. Technology must be used to optimize your outcomes. Improve your processes first – if you automate a bad process, it's still a bad process. However, you do need to incorporate technology to optimize your time and resources.

We have discussed the principles of digital transformation enough in this book for now. Plenty of other material is available elsewhere on transitioning to digital in HR. As for the top recommendations to focus on immediately, consider these immediate considerations:

- Shift to a cloud-based, open architecture structure. The cloud is easily accessible from anywhere, is just as (or more) secure than any other system, and is maintained without the need for ongoing upgrades.
- Use a platform instead of a product. People love communities where they can see their colleagues participating or engaging in a product or service. Just automating a product allows them access, but it's unidirectional. A platform provides the same product but also allows employees to engage with others and gain support.

- Make it user-focused. Just because *you* think it works well doesn't mean that your employees will. Ask questions and test your ideas outside of HR to avoid tunnel vision.
- Use business platforms that enable intelligent workflows across the enterprise. Bring in technical solutions that are so "cool" that managers won't be able to live without them. Just be sure they are helpful and provide more value than just their looks.
- Embed analytics and AI pervasively across all HR solutions. For example, implement bots, virtual agents, intelligent automation, and similar functions throughout HR platforms.

8. **Data Analytics**

We have also discussed the use of data several times. To get started as a priority, consider how to begin to measure what matters most. You will want to avoid measuring *everything*. That is just too much data. Instead, consider what you want to measure, how to measure it, and how you can have it presented in a way that will help you to manage the outcomes best.

To help, consider implementing the following:

- Significant investments in AI and analytics across HR. This will require integrating current software into a reporting process to deliver and report metrics. If possible, find a way to create a dashboard that provides real-time information to you, your team, and company leaders on your key metrics.

- Use a combination of structured and unstructured data. There are easy data available to measure – and there is more difficult (but important) data that is not as easy to measure and report. Consider what information is important but may be difficult to obtain and develop a strategy to collect measurable information on it periodically.
- Incorporate predictive analytics. Adopting forecasting into your metrics helps you not only understand what you have today but will also help you know what you and your business will need tomorrow.
- Leverage data from internal and external sources. Internal sources may come from company records, financial reports, and demand management projections. External data may come from labor market statistics, social media platforms, and the local journal of business.
- Apply insights to improve organizational performance and HR programs.

9. Reskill Your HR Team

Reskilling employees falls under professional development. Reskilling your HR team deserves a section all its own. You cannot expect to lead the business if you do not hold the tools to be able to do so. Your team must continuously improve their abilities to lead and develop others. Shifting into its transformational role, HR 3.0 will require HR team members to achieve greater levels of competence. As they do, HR can:

- Become transformation advisors to executives on how to implement and enhance business strategy.
- Align increased HR expertise with broader business acumen to improve the quality of talent sourcing.
- Focus primary services on meeting the immediate needs of senior business leaders.
- Be seen as trusted coaches, data-driven problem solvers, and change agents.
- Create new opportunities for the business to leverage the workforce strategically.

10. Get the Right Talent

Finally, an aligned HR 3.0 team can put its people, processes, and resources together to identify, source, and prepare the right talent for the business. Transformative HR can provide:

- Agile and optimized global hiring practices that predict and source according to market demands.
- Personalized experience-centric candidate journeys to optimize the candidate experience.
- Hyper-targeted sourcing by skills and interests to match the right people to the right position.
- Aggregation of social and digital tools to find the right people in the right places and attract them to the right opportunities.
- Focus on the employer brand and ensure alignment between new hires and delivering the promise you make within the employee experience.

The First Step Is Yours

Now it's time for you to do the rest by taking the first step. The day of transformation is here. Transformation begins with shifting your mindset. That change in mindset begins the moment you decide to become something new. Today can be that day – now can be that moment.

Begin right now to start the momentum and move forward immediately.

About the Author

Dr. Wade Larson

Dr. Wade is on a personal mission to help individuals and companies overcome mediocrity and achieve their best. Wade has worked with hundreds of organizations and thousands of individuals as an HR consultant and executive to develop programs that help them do more, achieve more, and be more.

As an international speaker and published author, Wade encourages leaders to improve their effectiveness in leadership and business. Wade has served as VP of HR and Chief HR Officer for several organizations. He owns Optimal Talent Dynamics where he works with companies and individuals to optimize talent solutions.

His first book, *Doing HR Better*, provides HR professionals a model to apply essential practices of process improvement to HR. In his second book, *Mind Shifts in Healthcare*, he introduces innovative solutions in wellness, benefits strategies, employee engagement, and cost containment to help change the culture around healthcare.

Wade earned his Bachelors Degree from Brigham Young University, his Masters Degree from Willamette University, and his Doctor of Management in Organizational Leadership from University of Phoenix. He also serves as faculty for Washington State University and Whitworth University.

For more information see www.WadeLarson.com

Citations

i Covey, Stephen R. 1989. *The Seven Habits of Highly Effective People: Restoring the Character Ethic.* New York: Simon and Schuster.
ii Kotter, J. P. (1996). Leading Change. Boston, Mass: Harvard Business School Press.
iii Drucker, P. F. (1999). *Management Challenges for the 21st Century.* New York: HarperBusiness.
iv Boutros, T., & Cardella, J. (2016). *The Basics of Process Improvement.* CRC Press: Boca Raton, FL.
v https://www.kotterinc.com/8-steps-process-for-leading-change/
vi https://www.ccl.org/articles/leading-effectively-articles/most-important-leadership-competencies/
vii https://hbr.org/2016/03/the-most-important-leadership-competencies-according-to-leaders-around-the-world
viii https://www.gallup.com/workplace/245999/weave-agility-throughout-corporate-culture.aspx
ix https://hbr.org/2015/12/proof-that-positive-work-cultures-are-more-productive
x Lewis, S. (2016). *Positive Psychology and Change: How Leadership, Collaboration, and Appreciative Inquiry Create Transformational Results.* John Wiley & Sons, Ltd.

www.ingramcontent.com/pod-product-compliance
Lightning Source LLC
Chambersburg PA
CBHW052310220526
45472CB00001B/52